The Spiritual Life

The Spiritual Life

RECOGNIZING THE HOLY

Robert Fabing, S.J.

Paulist Press
New York/Mahwah, N.J.

Scripture quotations are taken from *The Jerusalem Bible* copyright © 1966, 1967, 1968, 1985, by Darton, Longman and Todd Ltd., and Doubleday, a division of Random House, Inc., reprinted by permission of the publishers.

Cover photo: Robert Fabing, S.J.
Cover and book design by Lynn Else

Library of Congress Cataloging-in-Publication Data

Fabing, Robert, 1942–
The spiritual life : recognizing the holy / Robert Fabing.
    p. cm.
Includes bibliographical references.
ISBN 0-8091-4209-0 (alk. paper)
1. Spiritual life—Christianity. I. Title.

BV4501.3.F33 2004
248.4′82—dc22

                                                                    2003026949

Published by Paulist Press
997 Macarthur Boulevard
Mahwah, New Jersey 07430

www.paulistpress.com

Printed and bound in the
United States of America

Contents

"In so far as you did this to one of the least of these sisters and brothers of mine, you did it to me."
(Matt 25:40)

Author's Preface

I would like to dedicate this book to all of the Jesuits, religious sisters, and married men and women who have been a part of the Jesuit Institute for Family Life Network's counseling staffs over the last thirty years. Each joined one of our more than forty marriage counseling and family therapy centers because he or she believes in the content of this book. I thank them all for their service and their companionship.

I want to thank my mother and father for the simple, deep, faith-filled, and beautiful love that they have for me and for each other.

I also would like to thank my brother Jesuits—William Johnston, S.J., of Sophia University in Tokyo; William Barry, S.J., tertian director in Boston; and Walter Farrell, S.J., former tertian director in Detroit—and Sr. Lucy Malarkey for their time, concern, and helpful reading and comments during the preparation of this book.

Finally, I would like to thank Arthur Deex for his computer skills in the various preparatory drafts of this work.

Robert Fabing, S.J.
Los Altos, California

Introduction

For the past thirty years I have been working in the fields of the Lord, founding marriage counseling and family therapy institutes.

As of the 2004 writing of this book, in God's grace forty marriage counseling and family therapy institutes in California and Oregon make up the Jesuit Institute for Family Life Network (JIFLNET).

How did all of this come about? Some historical information concerning this is in order. I entered the Society of Jesus in the fall of 1960 in Los Gatos, California. In early 1962, while I was a second-year novice and nineteen years old, an unheard-of event occurred. The master of novices came to my cubic (a room where four novices were living separated by an eight-foot-high wall and curtains). He asked me if I wanted to go to San Francisco and have dinner with my father and mother at our home the upcoming Sunday.

The master of novices had a brother in San Francisco and wanted to have Sunday dinner with him and his family. Would I like to go with him and the head novice? The head novice and I would eat at my family home. The master of novices would eat at his brother's.

We would make the drive in silence. The head novice would drive. There was one proviso. I could go if I sat in the backseat of the car on the fifty-mile drive to San Francisco, kept my head down and my eyes closed in "modesty of the eyes" fashion, and said three rosaries on the way up and on the way back in silence. I said, "No problem!"

On the next Sunday this is what we did.

On the way up to San Francisco that Sunday afternoon from Los Gatos, we came into the southern extremity of "the city." This was the Westlake area, where many, many homes are right next to each other in neat long rows. Somehow for the period of about thirty seconds I found my head up and my eyes opening. I gazed out at the houses all in a row right next to each other. As this happened, I felt a presence of Christ within me saying, "Bob, do you see all the pain in those houses...in the living rooms, the kitchens, the bedrooms, the family rooms?" The Lord showed me the pain in those homes. I said in response, "Yes." The Lord continued, "They're not doing anything about this at St. Ignatius High School, where you went to high school. They're not doing anything about this at the University of San Francisco." I said, "I know." Christ within me said, "I want you to do something about this." I said, "OK."

All of that took about thirty seconds.

The next fourteen years of my life involved preparing to live out this experience. I moved from studies in United States history, to philosophy, to sociology, to psychology, and to theology. There were many, many hours of supervised marriage and family counseling until I became licensed.

I began doing marriage, family, and child counseling at the Jesuit Retreat House when I arrived there in the fall of 1976. I began to gather marriage counselors and family therapists who were interested in interfacing the event of psychotherapy with the history of ascetical theology in the church, especially that of St. Ignatius Loyola. So began the Jesuit Institute for Family Life Network.

Since then I have experienced the same movement of Christ as I did in the novitiate some forty years ago in founding each of these institutes. It is the same Christ, the same call. I have come to understand that it is Christ suffering on the cross now in my sisters and brothers who cries out to me from these houses and these homes. It is to Christ, asking to be comforted as he suffers here, that I and the laymen and women, Jesuits and sisters in this work are responding.

What is clear to me is that this is the idea, the desire, and the work of Christ. It is the desire of Christ that men and women live together in peace, that children and parents live in peace, and that homes be a place of love, nurturing, and peace for all.

I am surprised who God is in Christ. I am surprised at what God is concerned about. This is God's interest. And in following Christ I have come to learn who Jesus really is and what Jesus really cares about and wants for God's people. It is wonderful.

The "subtitle" of this JIFLNET work is "Counseling in the Jesuit Tradition." Over the years what this has come to mean is that the event of psychotherapy in human history has offered us the discovery of the unconscious. This simple insight has impacted ascetical theology in a way that the classical works "on the attainment of the moral virtues," "on the practice of Christian Perfection," and "on the changing of bad habits to good habits" have worked at.

The discovery of the unconscious as an active player in human behavior has afforded us an effective tool in our quest to understand ourselves and one another as we attempt to follow Christ. It is Jesus who is in charge of the meaning of human life, even the meaning of holiness, not you and I. And Jesus in Matthew 25 says, "If you give to these sisters and brothers of mine you give to me." In this, Jesus defines prayer, the lifting of our hearts and minds to God, as every move we make to share who we are and what we have with our brothers and sisters. This situates every move persons make in psychotherapy to share themselves with their spouse, their children, their parents, as prayer...lifting one's heart and mind to God.

In this the psychotherapeutic shows itself as the gift of "the examination of consciousness" of St. Ignatius Loyola's Spiritual Exercises and identifies itself as "counseling in the Jesuit tradition."

This integration is not simple, as you know, but it does reveal why Christ is so intent that this freedom, love, and peace be in the hearts of each of God's children.

As the Lord has said to us, "The truth will set you free."

It is this that has attracted so many laymen and women, Jesuits and sisters to be on the staffs of these institutes. The heart of the work is the sacrament of the Eucharist that we celebrate at each staff meeting. What we are doing is tending the broken Body of Christ in these families. Answering the call of Christ is what has formed this work and continues to inform it.

This book is an expression of this grace.

Robert Fabing, S.J.
Los Altos, California

PART ONE

The Spiritual Life

CHAPTER ONE

The Spiritual Life

When I was young, I played golf. A lot of golf! When I was thirteen years old, I played football, basketball, and baseball. At the end of my thirteenth year I gave up all sports to play only golf. For the next four years I played golf almost every day. At sunup I would start hitting shots from my hundred practice balls spilled out on the dewy grass. Over and over, over and over...morning till night. I became a good golfer.

Today I watched fifteen minutes of the European Golf Championship on British Broadcasting Corporation television. I was channel-surfing when I came upon the event. I watched the leader of the golf tournament play. He took two full practice swings before each shot. It struck me that here is a person who is a professional. He has given his entire life to the game of golf. He has hit millions upon millions of golf balls and has taken millions and millions of practice swings in his life. He is a champion, the best golfer in Europe, the best golfer in the United States, and now the best golfer in the world. This champion is taking two full practice swings before each shot. I began to reflect that maybe this is how it really is...maybe the real champion, the real professional, the real success is the person who does the real simple thing over and over and over again and again, and again...and so does it well...very well.

This is a surprise to anyone who has ever tried to do something well.

It is said that the classical guitarist Andres Segovia would practice the guitar eight hours a day. Six of those hours Segovia practiced the scales. Two hours of his practice time were reserved for the new piece or pieces he was to perform. Andres Segovia was a master classical guitarist. He practiced the do-re-me scales six hours a day!

What does this say? Does this say something to us about what it means to do something well? Does this say anything to us about what it means to do something at all? I believe it says that something done well is not done spontaneously or without practice. I believe it says that what looks easy has been the product of day-in, day-out work and practice. I believe it says, "Nothing works unless you make it work."

If this is true, it must say something about the spiritual life, and it must say something about human life in general.

The spiritual life for a Christian is living a life centered in God revealed to us as three Persons: the Father, Jesus, and the Holy Spirit: God the Creator, Jesus the Redeemer, and the Holy Spirit the Sustainer. The spiritual life for a Christian is the ongoing process of coming "to live as Jesus lived" (John 2:6).[1] If we are to apply these examples from the world of golf and music, the spiritual life must involve a great deal of practice, over and over, day in and day out, for one's entire life.

If this is true, and I believe it is, what is to be practiced over and over, day in and day out, until you get good at it? Until it becomes simple? As an answer, we could put on the table human behavior or good habits. One can derive from the reading of the Gospels, the life, death, and resurrection of Jesus, a rather clear picture of the behavior patterns of Christ. One could be inspired by the spirit of Jesus to act, or speak, or behave as Jesus did in the Gospels, for instance. In this one could attempt to "do as Jesus did" or "live as Jesus lived" or "behave as Jesus behaved" or "speak as Jesus spoke" or "act as Jesus acted."

One could try this. As one attempts to behave as Jesus did, one would succeed in certain circumstances and events and situations and fail in others. As one lives the spiritual life, one would become aware of what the musician, the artist, and the golfer quickly became aware of. "This is not so simple!" This can be difficult. It can be very difficult, and at times, it can feel impossible. As this perception emerges, one would begin to realize that one must attempt again and again in order to succeed. One would realize that one must have momentum to behave in a new way that belies perhaps years and years of unlike or unsympathetic behavior. This inertia is strong and deeply ingrained, perhaps from habitual behavior that is not consonant with the way one is aspiring to be. The momentum needed is the over-and-over-again habit of attempts and occasional successes. How is this momentum achieved? By trial and error...by attempt and failure...by trying and succeeding! By engaging in a behavior that one would like to be able to perform well, one becomes aware of what is involved: the perception of the reality that this is not simple to do.

As Scripture says, the whole law and the prophets can be summed up in this, "Love the Lord your God with your whole heart, your whole mind, and your whole self. And love your neighbor as yourself" (Mark 12:30). Here, as we know, love of neighbor is intimately linked with the love of God. This has been the deep Christian insight that has affected and molded much of our Western civilization.

This civilization of ours has been characterized throughout the centuries by theoretical and practical contributions to human evolution, ranging from Plato's philosophy to the invention of the computer. In the beginning of the twentieth century a phenomenon that has come to be called psychotherapy captured the minds and gripped the interest of people in the West. The rise of the study of psychology and psychotherapy has been so all-embracing that one may say that today the high priest of Western culture is the psychiatrist and the psychologist. The phenomenon of psychology deserves the interest, the attention, the dialogue, and entrance into the Christian reality and experience of spirituality.

Many Christians living the spiritual life consider prayer, God, and their movement toward God a Sunday affair. They feel their emotional lives, relationships, and problems have little to do with God. They feel that God is distant to their intimate concerns, and even more so do they feel that the church has abstracted itself from their concerns. They feel that they must suffer the deep emotional pain of their human relationships apart from the interest of God and the church. The psychiatric-psychological community speaks deeply to this loneliness; it speaks with concern, knowledge, and a helping ear. The discovery of the unconscious and the resulting knowledge of human psychology and psychiatry is a blessing for us. The rise of psychotherapy as a commonplace event is an advancement and much welcomed gift. There is a need now for

Christian resources regarding the spiritual meaning of emotional and psychotherapeutic suffering. There is a need to see the presence of God in one's unconscious and emotional psychotherapeutic encounter and experience. There is a need to see God's intimate concern that we love one another. There is a need to see how God wishes human beings to share their intimate, unconscious selves with one another. There is a need to see how the spiritual life, the psychotherapeutic experience, and the great commandment of God are really one event.

As we have been taught, the spiritual life, the moving toward God, a relationship with God, is prayer. There are many ways to pray and to move toward God. The problem is that many do not see the discovery of their unconscious and the resulting emotional suffering they endure and experience as movement toward God...as prayer. The problem is another statement of the classic problem of the body-soul dichotomy. The problem is the inability to see living daily human life and its emotional pain and resolution as holiness itself...as the spiritual life itself.

The direction and movement of this book is to see daily human life and our emotional suffering and resolution for what it actually is...as movement toward God...as prayer...as holiness...and as living the spiritual life itself. The purpose of this work is to unfold the meaning of the spiritual life and the meaning of emotional suffering in order to speak to those who see no meaning in their pain and thus to provide the reality of a healing effect.

In looking at the spiritual life of moving toward intimate union and intimacy with God, we can find a meaning in our life experience that brings a clarity and resultant freedom.

For centuries spiritual writers have analyzed the spiritual life into the purgative, the illuminative, and the unitive ways. They suggest that the purgative way takes many, many years and includes the *via negativa*. The *via negativa* comprises the decisions we make to give up various self-orientated behaviors and dynamics.

The illuminative way consists in our coming to know Jesus Christ, the image of "the God we have never seen" (John 1:18). This is done in us "by the Spirit" (2 Cor 3:18) attracting us to Christ. This way is many years in the making.

The unitive way comprises our life of intimacy with God, where our heart, mind, and behavior-body expressions are the living presence of the love of God in the world. This way occupies us for the rest of our lives.

This outline of the spiritual life has been handed down to us with the aura that one would spend the years from fifteen to thirty-five walking the *via negativa* of the purgative way. Then one would advance to the next stage of twenty years, the illuminative way, from thirty-five to fifty-five. Finally, one would spend the final years of fifty-five to seventy-five or eighty-five in the unitive way.

It may be slightly unfair to characterize this as a spiritual life worldview, but the literature suggests that this is, nonetheless, an accurate depiction of what was presented. We can now look at this model in light of all of the research on adult life cycles and stages and raise the following question: "Can I be in all three of these stages in my spiritual life at the same time? Can I be in the purgative way vis-à-vis one dynamic in my spiritual life while I am in the illuminative way in another, and at the same time be in the unitive way in another? I think the answer is "Yes."

My hope is that the significance of this journey will be in revealing that the emotional suffering moving through our lives in successfully experiencing our unconscious is the very meaning of holiness itself and so is a movement toward God and the very meaning of prayer itself. A whole dimension of power and support is added to the Christian traveler...the pilgrim...the sufferer...as one walks one's road. A person can derive a perception of how God wants one to do this...to share...to go through this emotional suffering of looking at one's unconscious. The added significance of God's support, union, and intimate care bolsters the intent of the Christian traveler. The significance here lies in the area of the individual Christian pilgrims' recognition that they are holy in their journey into their unconscious...that rather than being estranged from God and the Christian church and other human beings by going through and traveling through emotional suffering, they are embracing their real self, others, God, Christianity, and, indeed, holiness itself.

In embarking on this journey together, I am assuming the following:

- The individual pilgrim traveler involved in this parable-story or example believes in God and believes in the divinity of Jesus Christ of Nazareth.

- The church has resources and riches in its spiritual tradition and history. It can help uniquely and is obligated to aid persons going through their emotional suffering in their journey into their own unconscious.

- Individual Christians need the support of Christ and the church as they experience emotional suffering, and those individuals going through this suffering are searching for this additional strength and meaning not ordinarily available in our society.

In order that we may have a common understanding of certain key terms that I am using, I provide the following:

- emotional suffering: that emotional pain endured by persons as they experience their own unconscious and go through the process of freeing themselves from false-self experience and behavior and realize their own real-self experience and behavior.

- spirituality: the manner in which individuals image and understand God's relating to them and the manner in which individuals respond to and seek God.

- real self: "the original force toward individual growth and fulfillment" (Karen Horney).[2]

- idealized self: what we are in our irrational imagination... what we should be according to the dictates of neurotic pride (Karen Horney).[3]

- self-concept: the complexus of reality, value, and possibility assumptions individuals have of themselves, others, and the world.

- neurotic conflict: the real self versus the idealized self in response to reality stimulus.

- weakness: the inability to effect any creative significant change in one's situation; powerlessness as St. Paul explains it in his letters.

- dark night of the soul: the process described and explained by St. John of the Cross in his work by the same title.

In this exploration of the spiritual life I am also assuming the following:

- God wants us to share ourselves intimately with each other, and this sharing is a way of fulfilling the Great Commandment.

- Emotional knowledge and communication are necessary to facilitate real self-realization.

- Individuals leading the spiritual life need to see the meaning and presence of God in their emotional suffering.

- The church possesses a unique and positive role and heritage in this quest of individuals leading the spiritual life and experiencing emotional suffering as they move to finding God and their real-self life.

I am, therefore, attempting to unfold the nature and meaning of the spiritual life. God's will in the spiritual life is that we share our inner feelings with ourselves and with one another. With the rise in an awareness that we have an unconscious and an awareness of the emotional suffering involved, with the fact that talking about this is now a commonplace event, there is a need to see emotionality, human interaction, and the suffering that takes place in this experience and communication for the holiness it is.

There is a need to see emotional and psychological pain and suffering for what it is…as the spiritual life. The need here is to provide the context out of which one can articulate one's own inner event. This book aims to provide the opportunity to reflect on one's own inner experience. The object here is not cathartic per se. It is to engender reflection and prayer about your already felt experience so that you move toward conviction with respect to your own inner experience. The goal is for you to speak out and proclaim from your conviction and communicate to other human beings struggling with the same realities. As we know, experience comes first, then reflection on one's experience, then conviction (insight) from one's experience, and, finally, proclamation (communication) to others of what one has discovered.

My hope is to provide a context for you to place yourself within. My task is to present an understanding of the spiritual life in which you, the reader, can stand or place yourself to see where you are. I will use some questions for your reflection and discussion to assist in this unfolding. I hope to present an understanding of the spiritual life by using a parable-story of a traveler as an illustration from which to work. I ask you to reflect and pray and come to a perception of where you are in this continuum experience of the parable-story's traveler. In some ways this is a workbook. This perception will provide a balance and a stability consisting of self-understanding before God. From this foundation of understanding one obtains a firm stance for interacting with one's very self, with others, and with God. This self-understanding, this stability, is conviction. It is the freedom of the children of God. It is the true peace of being able to articulate one's own inner event.

I will use a dialectical method in this presentation on the spiritual life. I will present one dimension of a given dynamic, then present another, then present the bridge between them...the "in-between." Chapters 3 through 7 will present one dimension of the spiritual life: the human emotional or psychological experience. Chapters 8 through 10 will present the other dimension: the human experience interfacing with God. Chapters 11 through 15 will present the third and final consideration, the identification of these two dimensions as the spiritual life.

The method of presentation will be to pose questions for you to answer in the privacy of your prayer or in a group. The problem being addressed here is that of seeing God's presence in your emotional-psychological suffering...in the suffering entailed in moving from unconscious emotional-psychological conflict to conscious emotional-psychological resolution and health. Many do not perceive God's presence here or consider this journey as the spiritual life. Many pray earnestly to God on Sunday and feel that their emotional lives, relationships, and problems have little to do with God and their seeking of God.

Questioning, prayer, and reflection can deal with this in an effective way because prayer and reflection speak to body and spirit at the same time. Prayer and reflection destroy a body-spirit separation by their very nature. Prayer speaks to body and spirit simultaneously, thus destroying such a split. Because this is so, I have developed questions and prayer reflections to interpret and support the spiritual life. This furthers the purpose of this work. God wants us to communicate with each other. This is prayer; this is movement toward God; this is holy; this is the spiritual life.

I will be eclectic throughout this book, drawing from a variety of sources. These include the theories of personality of Karen Horney and Alfred Adler, and the spiritualities of St. Paul, St. John of the Cross, and St. Ignatius in order to formulate what it means to live a spiritual life.

In evolving a theory of emotion and emotional development, I will assume a metaphor or parable-story in which the emotion of anger will be the response to an experience of being frustrated. This is only one of many theories of emotionality. It is the one that I will explore in this work.

As Robert A. Harper, discussing the value of an eclectic outlook, put it:

> Blunt instruments are surely rendered no sharper by rigidity, dogmatism, and fanatic adherence to a particular system. Young therapists in training should be encouraged to expose themselves to the full range of therapeutic theories and to experiment with the complete repertory of therapeutic techniques. Such therapists, in this period which is hopefully a prelude to more scientific procedures, are more likely, we firmly believe, to be helpful to a great number of patients than therapists conditioned in one theoretical orientation and its limited techniques.[4]

In part 3 and part 4 I will be drawing on the spiritualities of St. Paul, St. John of the Cross, and St. Ignatius Loyola as resources for bringing to light the meaning of the spiritual life.

Discussion Questions

Do you think living the spiritual life takes practice over and over, again and again, daily? Why?

How do you experience this? Share in your groups or with another.

Do you think you can be in the purgative, the illuminative, and the unitive ways of the spiritual life all at the same time vis-à-vis different dynamics in your life? How can this be?

Do you believe you have an unconscious? What would it be? Why would anyone have an unconscious?

What would one want to become unaware of in life?

Does your unconscious play an active role in your spiritual life? How?

CHAPTER TWO

The Spiritual Life Historically

I believe the discovery of the unconscious to be one of the greatest developments of the twentieth century. The experience of emotionality has been deeply revealed to us as never before. This event, this phenomenon—the discovery of the human unconscious—emerges onto the stage of the history of the Christian spiritual life. What does this emergence mean to what we have considered the spiritual life to be?

We can engage this question by asking this: What have Christians living the spiritual life throughout the centuries considered the spiritual life to be? What does Christian history tell us is the meaning and scope of the spiritual life? If we can direct ourselves to these questions as we begin, we can see what the discovery of the unconscious reveals to us about the very meaning of the spiritual life itself.

If we look at some of the writings that have come down to us through the centuries of Christian history, we can come to an understanding of what the event of the discovery of the unconscious means to the spiritual life. Let us look at what the spiritual life means to saints of the church and to those who have dedicated their lives to looking intensely at and living the spiritual life.

I would briefly like to consider the following works: *The Imitation of Christ* by Thomas à Kempis, *The Practice of Perfection and Christian Virtues* by Alphonsus Rodriguez, S.J., *The Ascent of Mount Carmel* and *The Dark Night of the Soul* by St. John of the Cross, *The Interior Castle* by Teresa of Avila, and *The Divine Milieu* by Pierre Teilhard de Chardin, S.J.

These works today and in their own day were considered to be stellar exposés on the spiritual life. The subject matter that they deal with and the questions they raise reveal directly what the people of the author's time considered to be the realm of the spiritual life.

I invite you to journey back in time with me and visit what these great spiritual writers considered the spiritual life to be. I am asking you to enter into a contemplative reading of chapter titles from these works. Come with me and engage the historical world of the spiritual life.

Let's begin this contemplative reading by considering the thirteenth-century work *The Imitation Of Christ* by Thomas à Kempis. Consider what à Kempis meant by the spiritual life from these chapter titles of his work.

On inordinate affections.
The means to get peace and profit from good habits.
On the profit of adversity.
That we not too easily judge other's deeds.
On bearing others' faults.
On the humble acknowledgment of our own defects.
On the knowledge of ourselves.
Of the lack of solace and comfort.
That the desires of the heart ought to be well examined.
How one should order their self in their desires.
On the acknowledgment of our own infirmities.
On the liberty, excellence, and worthiness of freedom.
Against the sayings of detractors.
Against the vain judgments of men and women.
How one should rule their self in outward things.
That one should not be importunate in their business.
That men and women are not always to be believed because
    they so easily offend in words.
That one should not be too much cast into discouragement
    though one happen to fall into some defects.
On the searching of our own conscience.[5]

Do any of these chapter titles strike a bell in you? Do any of these titles pique your interest? If they do, why would that be? Could it be that you or someone you know may be experiencing now a similar dynamic? What does this say to you about the meaning of the spiritual life? How are you reacting now? Pause and reflect.

Let us move into considering the writings of Alphonsus Rodriguez. For over four hundred years the church presented to its flock the writings of this sixteenth-century Spanish Jesuit as a classic model of the spiritual life. His work, *The Practice of Perfection and Christian Virtues*, was considered to be the authoritative compendium of the very meaning of the spiritual life. Consider the treatise titles:

The First Treatise

On the affection and desire that we should have for virtue and perfection.

That a desire of growing and going forward in self-improvement is a great sign of one's being in the grace of God.

On the perseverance we ought to have in virtue.[6]

The Second Treatise

On the perfection of our ordinary actions.

That our advancement and perfection consists in doing ordinary actions well.

On other means which is to do every action as if it were to be the last of our life.

On another means of doing our actions well which is to take no account of anything beyond today.[7]

The Third Treatise

On the integrity and purity of intention we ought to have in all our actions.[8]

The Fourth Treatise

On union and fraternal love.

Of the need we have of this love and union and of some means to preserve us in the same.

That we ought to be much on our guard against biting words that may offend our brother or sister or give them any displeasure.

That we ought to beware of wrangling, contradicting, and rep-
rehending.

On what we are to do when we have had any passage of arms
or disagreement with our brother or sister.

On three directions to be observed when another has given us
some occasion of annoyance.

On rash judgments, explaining in what their malice and gravity
consists.

On the causes and roots whence rash judgments proceed, and
their remedies.[9]

Do any of these titles challenge you now? The spiritual-life language and the expressions used reflect the sixteenth-century world
of the author. What about the experiences that these titles refer to?
Do they refer to some of your experiences? Pause and reflect.

Let us continue a meditative reading.

The Seventh Treatise

The importance of examination of consciousness.

On what subjects the particular examen should be made.

On two important pieces of advice how to hit upon and choose
the right subject for particular examen.

That the examen of consciousness is a means of putting into
execution all other spiritual methods and directions, and
the reason why we do not profit by it is that we do not
make it as we ought.[10]

The Eighth Treatise

On the conformity to the Will of God.

On the conformity that we should have to the Will of God in
the distribution of natural gifts and talents.

On the conformity that we should have to the Will of God in
times of sickness.

On the conformity we should have to the Will of God in death
as in life.

On the conformity which we should have to the Will of God in
the general afflictions and calamities of our lives.

On the means that will help us much to bear with afflictions.[11]

How are you doing? Are you hanging in there? Has it occurred to you why it is that such subjects are dealt with in a work on the spiritual life? What do you think? Look at what is considered here as the spiritual life. Pause and reflect.

Remember that these subjects gripped the minds and hearts of those during the sixteenth century and for four hundred years after its writing. Let us continue.

The Ninth Treatise

That we must join mortification to prayer and that these two things must help one another.

In what mortification consists, and the need in which we stand of it.

That one of the greatest chastisements of God is to give a person over to their appetites and desires, abandoning them so that they go after them.

That our spiritual advancement and perfection consists in mortification.

That they who make no effort to mortify themselves do not live the life of a spiritual being.

How the exercise of mortification ought to be put in practice.

That we should chiefly mortify ourselves in that vice or passion which has the greater sway over us and makes us fall into our greatest fault.

Of a motive that will facilitate and make agreeable the practice of mortification: the hope of reward.[12]

Does any of this sound familiar? The consideration of these dynamics and experiences comprise the spiritual life. What do you think? Pause and reflect.

The next two treatises deal with self-knowledge and temptation, respectively. What do these considerations bring into your purview as you read them?

The Eleventh Treatise

On the Excellence of the virtue of humility and the need we have of it.

On self-knowledge as the root, and the sole and necessary means to attain humility.

That humility is the foundation of all virtues.

How we should so exercise ourselves in self-knowledge as not to be discouraged or lose confidence.

Of the good things and great advantages that there are in the exercise of self-knowledge.

That self-knowledge does not bring discouragement, but rather courage and strength.

How much it behooves us to exercise ourselves in self-knowledge.

That humility is the means to attain true peace of soul, and we shall never arrive at that without it.

Of the other manner of means more effectual for gaining the virtue of humility: by practicing it.

How we are to make the particular examen on the virtue of humility.

That humility is the means to overcome all temptations and obtain the perfection of all virtues.[13]

The Twelfth Treatise
On temptation in this life.

Of benefits and advantages that temptations bring with them.

That temptations avail us greatly to know ourselves, and have recourse to God.

That in temptations we are proved and purified, and take root better in virtue.

That in temptations one learns lessons not for oneself only, but for others.

On remedies against temptations.

Reasons for fighting with great courage and confidence under temptation.

That in different temptations we should behave differently.[14]

What do you think? What are you experiencing now as you consider this treatment? These titles refer to experiences considered part of the spiritual life. What do you think?

The following treatises deal with joy and sadness, with having a spiritual guide and dealing openly with that person, and with the need for bringing up and sharing issues that are a source of conflict with others.

The Fourteenth Treatise
On joy and sadness.
On the great problems that follow from sadness.
On the roots and causes of sadness and its remedies.
On other very ordinary roots of sadness.
That there is such a thing as good sadness.[15]

The Twenty-Third Treatise
On the manifestation of conscience.
How important and necessary it is to deal openly with the one who guides us.
What a great relief and consolation it is for one to be open with the one who guides us.
Some first answers to the difficulties that usually hinder this openness in manifestation.
Meeting the main difficulty that is apt to stand in the way of openness in manifestation.[16]

The Twenty-Fourth Treatise
On fraternal correction.
That correction is a mark of love, and the great good there is in it.
That pride is the cause of our not taking correction well.
On the inconveniences and losses that follow from not taking correction well.
How important it is to take correction and admonition well.[17]

There is presented to us a broad spectrum of human experience here. Do you think it is proper to consider this as part of the spiritual life? Why? Pause and reflect.

The sixteenth-century Carmelite priest St. John of the Cross is a Doctor of the Church because of his writing on the spiritual life. He wrote four major works, *The Ascent of Mount Carmel, The Dark Night of the Soul, The Living Flame of Love,* and *The*

Spiritual Canticle. The Ascent of Mount Carmel engages the spiritual life in terms of beginning stages. This work deals with the actions that we ourselves can do as we begin to follow Christ. He brings to light that in the beginning of our spiritual life we are the ones in charge of what we do.

The Dark Night of the Soul concerns what God induces within us as we travel our spiritual life. *The Living Flame of Love* takes up the human experience of union with God in love. And, finally, *The Spiritual Canticle* looks at the entire flow and experience of the spiritual life.

Let yourself free-associate as you slowly and meditatively read these chapter titles of *The Ascent of Mount Carmel.*

Book One

The nature of the dark night through which a soul journeys to divine union.

The necessity of truly traversing the dark night of sense mortification of the appetites in journeying toward union with God.

Proofs from passages of sacred scripture for the necessity of journeying toward God through this dark night, the mortification of the senses and the appetites.

How the appetites torment a person.

Proofs of how freedom from all appetites is necessary to attain divine union.

An explanation of the kinds of appetites which can bring harm upon a soul.

The manner and method of entering this night of the senses and appetites.[18]

What is happening within you as you read these titles? What are you experiencing ? Where is your associating taking you?

Keeping in mind your reactions, let us proceed to a consideration of some of the chapter titles of *The Dark Night of the Soul.* Move into this in a prayerful way as above.

Book One

The imperfections of beginners.

Some of the imperfections of pride possessed by beginners.

Some of the imperfections of avarice commonly found in beginners.

The imperfections of lust usually found in beginners.

The imperfections of the capital vice of anger into which beginners fall.

Imperfections of gluttony, envy, and sloth.[19]

What are you experiencing as you read this? Do these titles seem to
you to be encompassed in what you mean by "the spiritual life"? I
invite you to write down your own reactions in a notebook as we
proceed.

In taking up the work of the sixteenth-century Carmelite nun
St. Teresa of Avila, I remember my time in that ancient walled city.
Avila is the only extant walled city in Spain. It is beautiful. It is here
that the drama of the life of Teresa unfolded. It was in Avila that
Teresa suffered much in founding a reformed Discalced Carmelite
tradition. She knows of what she writes as forces and dynamics rose
up from seemingly nowhere to oppose her.[20] "No foundation was
made without trouble. What it is to have to contend against many
minds! I never refrained from making a foundation for fear of trouble. It was my lack of health that most frequently wearied me. The
weather was so severe, and I, so sickly."[21]

The work of hers that we look at now is *The Interior Castle*.
This book by Teresa depicts the human journey to God—the spiritual life—as moving through various dwelling places or rooms or
mansions within a castle. For Teresa of Avila, "the journey to God
in *The Interior Castle* and the journey to self are the same journey."[22]

The first three dwelling places or mansions (1, 2, and 3)[23] represent all the things we can do in the spiritual life. These include the
decisions we make as we live the spiritual life. We are, as it were, in
charge as we proceed toward God.

The next three dwelling places or mansions (4, 5, and 6)[24] represent the experiences in the spiritual life that are out of our hands.
Here God is in control, and we are not. The seventh and final
dwelling place or mansion within *The Interior Castle* speaks of the
spiritual union of intimacy we can have with God.

Meditatively consider various chapter titles from the first three
dwelling places to see what Teresa meant by the spiritual life.

The First Dwelling Place
The Beauty and Dignity of Our Souls.
The Benefit That Comes from Understanding This Truth.
The Importance of Self-Knowledge and Matters Concerning
This Theme.[25]

The Second Dwelling Place
The Importance of Perseverance in the Struggle against
Temptation.[26]

The Third Dwelling Place
On the Little Security We Have in Our Human Lives and on
How We Should Deal with This.
Dryness in Prayer and the Method of Looking at One's Life
during This Experience.[27]

"Teresa reminds us that we do not go to God by losing ourselves,
but by finding ourselves. She stresses the need for humility which is
another way of saying that we must be anchored in reality. This reality is a knowledge and acceptance of ourselves."[28] Do these chapter
titles from Teresa evoke any questions within you? Is interior beauty
a concern of the spiritual life? Is understanding the truth of the dignity of your spiritual life important to you? Is self-knowledge important to you in your spiritual life? Do you have a method of reflecting
on the health of your spiritual life? What are your reflections? Pray
on these themes and questions.

The Fourth Dwelling Place
Discusses the difference between consolations or the feelings of
Tenderness in prayer and other spiritual delights.[29]

The Fifth Dwelling Place
The kind of union the soul can reach with God's help and of
how Important love of one's sisters and brothers is for
union with God.[30]

The Seventh Dwelling Place
Treats of how the soul and human person are one.[31]

"Teresa locates the religious call and the psychological call in the one call coming from God who is center to a person's existence....[32] The religious journey and the psychological journey are one journey in Teresa's experience."[33] What is this deep woman of faith engendering in you now, four hundred years after she wrote about the meaning of the spiritual life? Do you have feelings of tenderness in you prayer? What is the relationship between love of our sisters and brothers and union with God? Do you think the psychological journey and the religious journey are one journey? Reflect on your prayerful experience.

This consideration does not exhaust, or even touch, the vast resources of writing on the spiritual life that exist for us in our Christian tradition. Our purpose here is not to survey this entire body of material but simply to choose writings of significant figures that would assist us in seeing what the spiritual life is. This method will tell us in some way what at least these great figures in the spiritual life consider the spiritual life to be. That, I believe, will be very helpful in our investigation.

In taking up a more recent writer on the spiritual life, Pierre Teilhard de Chardin, we move into the mid–twentieth century. Teilhard was a French Jesuit priest whose life spanned the first half of the twentieth century. He was a paleontologist. This profession occupied his life as a deep call within a call. The work of his that we are considering here is *The Divine Milieu*, an essay on the meaning of the spiritual life.

Let us look at the chapter titles he considers:

The Divination of Our Activities
The Christian Problem of the Sanctification of Action
All Endeavour Cooperates to Complete the World in Christo Jesu
In Our Universe All That Is Sensible Exists for the Soul
Communion through Action
Detachment through Action
The Divination of Our Passivities
The Christian Perfection of Human Endeavour
The Passivities of Growth[34]

Teilhard writes:

> Indeed, Lord, it will be—by virtue of a claim which you yourself have implanted at the very center of my will! I desire and need that it should be.
>
> I desire it because I love irresistibly all that your continuous help enables me to bring each day to reality. A thought, a material improvement, a harmony, a unique nuance of human love, the enchanting complexity of a smile or a glance, all these *new* beauties that appear for the first time, in me or around me, on the human face of the earth—I cherish them like children....
>
> The more I examine myself, the more I discover this psychological truth: that no one lifts his little finger... [without building], your work, my God.[35]

What are you experiencing as you begin to become aware of what Teilhard is referring to in these chapter headings and quotes? Areas of human actions? All of our human endeavors? Your sensible life? Your own growth?

We continue our contemplative reading of Teilhard's chapter titles:

Our Struggle with God against Evil
Our Apparent Failure and Its Transfiguration
True Resignation
Attachment and Detachment: First Develop Yourself
The General Rhythm of Christian Life: Development and
    Renunciation
The Meaning of the Cross
The Spiritual Power of Matter
The Coming of the Divine Milieu: The Taste for Being
Individual Progress in the Divine Milieu: Purity, Faith, Fidelity
Collective Progress in the Divine Milieu: Love[36]

Quoting Teilhard here exposes for us a central insight into the meaning of the spiritual life. He says:

Why separate and contrast the two natural phases of a single effort? Your essential duty and desire is to be united with God. But in order to be united you must first of all be—be yourself as completely as possible. And so you must develop yourself and take possession of the world in order to be. Once this has been accomplished it is time to accept diminishment for the sake of being in another. Such is the sole and twofold precept of complete Christian asceticism.[37]

These harmonise, like breathing in and out in the movement of our lungs...two phases of the soul's breath. This is the solution. From this dynamic point of view the opposition so often stressed between asceticism and mysticism disappears. There is no longer any reason to distinguish between an ascetic and mystic once the movement toward the human center and the divine center are seen as one.[38]

As you read these chapter titles and quotes, what are you experiencing? Your struggling against evil? Your experience of failure? Your acceptance of the lowly in your life? Your acceptance of yourself and who you are in the world? Are any of these dynamics and realities gripping you in your life now? These issues and areas of our lives Chardin considers to be the spiritual life. Do you consider these areas and experiences and issues to be your spiritual life?

Discussion Questions

When you hear the phrase "the spiritual life," what does that bring to mind for you?

What would you say Thomas à Kempis considered the spiritual life to be?

What was Alphonsus Rodiguez's view of the spiritual life?

What was the view of St. John of the Cross?

What did Teresa of Avila depict the spiritual life to encompass?

What did Pierre Teilhard de Chardin consider the spiritual life to be?

What other historical figures have presented you with an expression of the spiritual life? Who were they? What did they consider the spiritual life to have been?

Share your reflections in your group.

PART TWO

Self-Knowledge

CHAPTER THREE

The Dark Night at Its Origin

In pondering the questions posed throughout the last chapter on the spiritual life, you may have reflected on your own contemporary experience and concluded that what à Kempis was referring to in the 1200s is the same suffering of injury and wrong that you are experiencing today eight hundred years later, and that the sadness and joy referred to by Rodriguez in the 1500s is the same sadness and joy that you are experiencing today six hundred years later.

The deep human emotional experiences referred to by these spiritual-life writers are indeed addressed today in our society as well. New insights have been given to us in our time. How do we deal with these deep human emotions today? How do we speak of these experiences today? I would like to reflect with you in the next five chapters on our own contemporary dealings with these experiences of the spiritual life.

In my work with women and men from all walks of life, from many and varied backgrounds, from a variety of cultures and countries around the world, a pattern began to arise uniting them. In their forties and early fifties, married and single men and women and priests and sisters have been coming to see me concerning a deeply felt confusion in their spiritual lives. Over and over again the same pain was emerging, needing to be dealt with. It was the same kind of "loss of direction," the same anguish, the same experience of suffering.

After I accompanied them through the process of this long "dark night," a pattern began to emerge concerning the journey. I have chosen to express the similarities of their experience by writing a parable-story that, I hope, will include as many as possible of the elements and dimensions and experiences of these travelers toward God yet remain true to a story line. I believe this parable to be a matrix or a horizon for you to hold your experience up against.

To begin with, it was abundantly clear that the origin of these travelers' suffering was more than their contemporary life experience. In our journey together it became obvious that this present suffering had its roots in the very beginning of their lives. It is there that this pattern began, and it is there that this parable-story will begin.

In this parable-story about the spiritual life, I will touch upon the spectrum of causal factors for such suffering, describing a typical way that such an experience begins. The theories and findings of Karen Horney and Alfred Adler will form the basis of this parable. The methodology will be one of tracing and describing a typical sequence of the development involved in such suffering. This will take in the origins and the re-creative causes involved. This story will mention a variety of symptoms and reactions but will be specific in selecting a typical pattern with specific symptoms and reactions.

Even though all of us every now and then will exhibit some of these symptoms that need to be resolved, this parable-story is meant to simply be a resource for your reflection.

The basic theoretical pattern I will develop is that in the process of human growing, individuals are faced with a frustration. There is a barrier to fulfilling their need and desire. This frustration will concern a traumatic interpersonal experience in our story. This frustrating ongoing experience will become the object of anger. Such feelings of anger will become the source of guilt feelings. The exact nature and development of these feelings, I hope, will become clear as we proceed. With guilt feelings imbedded and springing from their real self, they now begin to learn and build a system of defenses that will be a constructed barrier between their real-self feelings and the traumatic experience. To protect themselves from the experience of facing themselves as an angry person, they repress their anger, and then their guilt feelings subside. The defense system syndrome then becomes a pattern or a habit of interior behavior.

The question at hand now is, "What are the causes of such a painful feeling and disorder?" A definition of terms is in order. What do I mean by causes? By *causes* of such a habit I mean the factors originating in the self-concept of an individual that are contrary to the individual's real, basic, and radical self plus the interpersonal elements that cause and re-create these factors. By *self-concept* I mean the reality, value, and possibility assumptions persons make about who they are, about others, and about their world. I will, then, consider the dynamics involved in forming the self-concept. Since this suffering and pain are results of this pattern and habit of behavior, I will show how the disorder of the self-concept that is the source of this habit came to be.

It typically begins during early childhood. Alfred Adler's theory establishes this context:

> From the moment of birth a baby seeks to connect...itself with its mother. This is the purpose of its movements. For many months the baby's mother plays overwhelmingly the most important role in a baby's life: It is almost completely dependent upon her...the mother gives her baby the first contact with another human being, the first interest in someone other than itself.[39]

Children are deeply involved in establishing themselves as a "truster" interpersonally.[40] A child's process of breaking out into the world of reality is conditioned greatly by the degree to which the individual child knows itself as trusted and trusting. A mother, the primal, significant other, has the task of loving the child in such a way as to send the message to the child that it is OK to come out into reality and society and to be...OK to trust another in reality. "In the growth of this vision of society the most vital factor is the mother, as we have seen, for it is in its mother that every child makes its first contact with a trustworthy other..."[41]

The child now in early childhood depends completely on the significant other for its emotional survival. What this means is that the child is involved in its first step toward forming and establishing a self-conceptual life. If a child is accepted and loved by its significant other, that is, if the mother does issue the message that it is OK for the child to be itself, the child will develop healthy emotional patterns.

> The immense importance of the mother in this respect can be clearly recognized. She stands on the threshold of the

development of social feeling. The biological heritage of human social feelings is entrusted to her charge...her relations with the child, her knowledge, and her aptitude are decisive factors....We probably owe to the maternal sense of contact the largest part of human social feeling, and along with it the essential continuance of human civilization.[42]

What could go wrong? Obviously, the mother could harm the child's development by somehow not issuing this message of "okayness" to the child. "She can strengthen or hinder contact by the help she gives the child in little things, in bathing the child, in providing all that a helpless infant is in need of."[43] For example, let us say that the mother openly rejects the child; that is, she doesn't feed the child regularly or even strikes the child for crying. The mother does this consistently. The child's reaction can be traumatic in nature.[44]

For the purpose of this story, the reaction will be of such a nature. By this I mean that the level of influx of exciting stimuli is too high for the child's mental and emotional apparatus to stabilize.[45] There results an emergency in the emotional order. Organization and balance between the real emergent self and the self-concept life (the complexus of reality, value, and possibility assumptions) are disturbed.[46] What is involved here?

The entire emotional growth pattern is a constant attempt to align one's self-concept to one's real self. Karen Horney theoretically considers this in the following manner:

> The actual self is an all-inclusive term for everything that a person is at a given time: body and soul, healthy and neurotic. We have it in mind when we say that we want to know ourselves; i.e. we want to know ourselves as we are. The idealized self is what we are in our irrational imagination, or what we should be according to the dictates of neurotic pride. The real self, which I have defined several times, is the "original" force-toward individual growth and fulfillment, with which we may again achieve full identification when freed of the crippling shackles of neurosis.[47]

I will be using these distinctions as we proceed. The only question under consideration is whether one's self-concept will be formed correctly in a healthy way or incorrectly in a disordered way. If it is formed correctly, one's actual self—one's self-concept and one's real self—will be one and the same. If it is formed incorrectly, one's real self will be at war with one's idealized self-concept. The entire emotional-psychological growth pattern is an attempt to form a correct self-concept, to have the self-concept exactly the same as the real self. The self-concept is the platform from which one relates to the whole world.

One's self-concept is the sum total of what I think I am...what I think about myself and the world, and what I think I can do and be. Of course, this is a lifelong developmental task and it never really is complete. A child, then, is involved in establishing for itself a self-concept that is as close to its real self as the child can achieve. This is a process of continuous alignment and realignment. I would like to call such attempts at alignment "tasks." I have said that one task is to see oneself as a truster and trusted. But now the significant other who can build into the child such a feeling by a warm, unconditional, loving relationship rejects the child. For the child there is a frustration, a barrier. The child needs to be free-flowing with its parents.[48] The emotional-psychological survival of the child depends on this fulfillment.[49] One's self-concept formation depends on this acceptance. If it doesn't come, what is the result?

The child now experiencing an influx of nonwarmth and nonacceptance cannot fight it off directly; the child "spits it out," as it were. The child is experiencing a flood of stimuli that it cannot handle, a trauma. The first message that the child takes in is, "It's not OK to go out there." This means that the real self of the individual cannot come out.

> A wide range of adverse factors in the environment can produce this insecurity in the child: direct or indirect domination, indifference, erratic behavior, lack of respect for the child's individual needs, lack of real guidance, disparaging attitudes, too much admiration or the absence of it, lack of reliable warmth, having to take sides in parental disagreements, too much or too little responsibility, overprotection,

isolation from other children, injustice, discrimination, unkept promises, hostile atmosphere, and so on and so on.[50]

This means that a child, unsupported by significant affection, cannot form and establish a free relationship between its real self and reality.[51] This relationship is to become the self-concept. The frustration remains. A child continues to exist. The question is how does the child exist?

Two things occur immediately. First of all, the child has a direct reaction to the frustration—in this story, the mother. The significant other is now a hated significant other because it is in the way of the child's fulfillment. The second occurrence pertains to the "fulfillment" notion. The child now, realistically, knows itself as a "hater." The child is angry. This is a gut emotion, a real-self emotion. As I have mentioned, the primary task is to establish oneself as a truster. An angry "hater" notion of oneself does not congruently contribute to the "truster" task.[52] What results? The real self is very angry at not being unconditionally loved by its mother, but the child cannot let this come to the surface; the child does not have enough ego strength to allow itself to know itself as an angry hater. In effect, it's now not OK to be oneself. It is not a trusting quality. This can and does occur on a less than conscious level.[53] But a child still needs to establish a self-concept, needs to think of itself as loving and trusting. What does a child do? It develops an idealized self-concept. The individual develops a self-concept without the help of one's real self because it is not OK to be angry and let one's real self exist. The real self doesn't play an active role in creating and establishing the self-concept. The child now establishes its self-concept—assumptions of itself, assumptions concerning value and those concerning possibilities—without the help of its real self.

Karen Horney here considers this as an "idealized image":

A further attempt, here to be described, is the creation of an image of what the neurotic[s] believe...[themselves] to be, or of what at the time...[they feel they] can or ought to be. Conscious or unconscious, the image is always in large degree removed from reality, though the influence it exerts on the person's life is very real indeed.[54]

From this frame of reference—this self-concept, which is an idealized self-concept—the individual acts, behaves, and operates in the world. This complex of assumptions forms the starting point of all performance and behavior. The crucial question in development is to what degree this frame of reference, which is the source of so much of one's activity, is in congruence with one's actual self. Our story has started a motion of incongruence. The self-concept has started a "moved away" and idealized formation. This "moving away" is the direct result of the traumatic experience of being rejected. The flood of disorganizing rejection and the shock of having it come from the significant other overpowered the undefended real self of the child.[55] How did the child handle the shock of the traumatic experience, the flood of frustration and offensive emotion?

Two dynamics that play upon each other during development are present and operating. The first is the suppression of anger and hostility. The angry aspect of the individual is covered up. The second dynamic is that which is covering up. The anger or hostility that exists seeks expression by appending itself to its cause. But because "it's not good" to be angry with one's mother, because of the psychological survival of the child, the child cannot express this anger directly to its mother. The reason is the child's fear that if the child does express this anger, the mother will abandon it emotionally, so inducing a death to further fulfillment. The child therefore adjusts by accepting a halfway relationship with its mother. That is, the child will give her its "idealized self-conceptual activity" but will never give her its "real-self presence and feeling." This is the message behind the "It's not OK out there" statement. The child now operates in such a way, stimulated to be a truster by the significant other but knowing and feeling as an angry hater. As this concept seems to become deeper and more active, consciousness perceives it, and a feeling of guilt arises. This feeling of guilt originates from the perception of the angry feeling in the real self and the separating orientation of the idealized self-concept within the individual. This is basically an emotional perception at this age of an individual's growth. What is this guilt feeling like? This feeling is one of self-hatred.[56] The exact object of the guilt feeling, typically, is the basic-real-self anger felt against the mother who is now the "unfulfiller."

The child now suppresses the feelings of anger it originally felt because the child feels that "it's not good" to feel such hostility to the person it needs such love from. Implicit in this statement is the self-effacing message that "I'm not good because I am angry because this anger of mine is why I am being rejected by my mother. My anger is making me unlovable."

Discussion Questions

When in the spiritual life you discover a problem affecting you, can you look at yourself for contributing elements?

Can you look to the birthplace in you of these dimensions? How so?

Does God call to you in grace to change your bad habits to good habits? How does God do this?

In order to do this, do you need to go to the birthplace of your bad habits?

Is a bad self-concept a bad habit? Why?

Does God want you to have an image of yourself that is based on who you really are?

The birth experience of this "bad habit" becomes unconscious. Does God want this to be unconscious?

Does God work to bring your unconscious to consciousness? How?

Does anger make you unlovable? Why?

CHAPTER FOUR

The Dark Night of Repression

As children develop, they come continually in contact with reality in many ways. This contact calls up the individual's self to meet it and interact with it. Now the child of our parable-story has two "selves" to be called up by a meeting with reality. Which one is the child going to "let out"? Not the real self because "it's not OK to go out there." Not the real self because the real self is angry...and "that's bad." Then what does the child let out as its self? Its idealized self-concept. This self-concept is reality assumptions and conclusions such as "I can't be myself. I must be great"; "It's not OK out there"; "I'm not good, it's not good to be me, but I should be good"; "I am unlovable, and it's my fault"; "I cannot trust my real self"; "I cannot trust my need for love!"; I cannot trust my real self"; "I cannot go to my real self inside in safety for feeling and information in interacting with the world"; "I feel I am unlovable." It cannot be acceptable and is not acceptable to a child to feel like this, so the child runs to escape contact with reality. This contact with reality is what is calling up the self from the individual. It is the conflict of selves coming to the fore that the child cannot experience because it is too painful. The conflict between one's real self and what one has come to believe and conclude about one's real self—one's self-concept—is very painful. The reason the conflict exists is that a gap between one's real self and one's idealized self-concept exists.[57] The individual fears that the real self may emerge as angry. This conflict causes a bodily reaction: anxiety. The individual is scared to death to feel this conflict coming up or to experience it. What does the child do? The child escapes into a world further removed from reality. By fleeing reality, the child escapes the pain by removing the possibility of conflict that reality will call up.

The manner in which a child proceeds to block the arising situation of meeting reality is called a defense mechanism.[58] A defense mechanism is an attempt to release and discharge the anxiety resulting from opposed impulses.[59] The opposing impulses, typically, are the notion of the individual held by the idealized self-concept and the existing real self. The self-concept has had one job since the moment of trauma, and that job was to "not be an angry person"…to run from the real self because the real self is "bad" and "dangerous." The "go force" or establishing force behind the development of the incorrect self-concept has been mistrust, anger, and hostility. What conclusions and what type of self-concept could be evolved by such motivation? One of "I have to" and "should." That is to say, because one's real self could not be included to any great degree in the self-concept formation, the self-concept had to try to be like the real self without allowing the real self to take its position of emerging dominance and existence in the self-concept formation.[60]

The inaccurate self-concept now overcompensates. It has to be trusting and loving. The notion of "must" in this statement implicitly includes an absence of the desired goal of natural development. This is true because the real self is not involved in trusting relationships. It is deficient and inadequate and needy. To cover up this feeling of inadequacy, the self-concept adopts for itself an attitude of demanding necessity to trust people.[61] In reality this is an attempt of the self-concept to build itself as far away as possible from the real self, who is "angry and hating."

What happens when the child of our parable-story with this condition comes in contact with reality? Two selves come to the fore, as has been said, but they come to the fore in conflict.

> The warded off instincts exert a constant pressure in the direction toward motility. Deprived of their possibility for direct discharge, they use any opportunity for indirect discharge, displacing their energy to any other impulse that is associatively connected with them, increasing the intensity of this substitute impulse or even changing the quality of the affect connected with it. Such a substitute impulse is called a derivative.[62]

The child's real self and the child's self-concept come to reality with opposite impulses. This conflictual experience yields anxiety at the perception of the child's internal disorganization. The child, then, must stop contact with reality, which is calling up the two selves. Defense-mechanismic behavior is unconsciously used and developed by the child as a barrier to hold off reality so that anxiety can be reduced, stabilized, and anesthetized by the child.

The use of defense-mechanismic behavior is a manner of handling the anxiety felt. This anxiety is overtly caused by the conflict in an individual from allowing the self to act from two frames of reference. The individual feels vague anxiety when acting from a maladaptively learned set of self-conclusions.

The child is deathly afraid to act from its real self as a frame of reference because of its angry-hateful hidden feelings, as they will endanger the child's need for the love of its mother. How does the individual alleviate this anxiety? How does the person handle it? By defense-mechanismic behavior such as escaping into or from reality, escaping into fantasy, rationalization of one's behavior, or projection of one's real-self feelings onto others. One can engage in repression of one's real-self feeling, a reaction that assumes ideas and attitudes that are contrary to the individual's real-self feeling, compensating for inadequacy by excelling in some other area, the displacement of one's real-self feeling onto some other object rather than one's mother, and regression into an earlier developmental level where the individual was and can be unthreatened. All these are ways of behaving that attempt to relieve the anxiety that occurs when the child feels the rising of the conflict between the idealized self-concept and the real self trying to represent the child to reality. Again, this conflict is another way of expressing fear of the appearance of the real-self feeling of anger and need for the child's mother.[63]

What happens if the behavior pattern learned from our parable-story environment is not enough to release all of the anxiety felt? This child chooses the behavior pattern of repression as a defense mechanism. The child simply will not allow the real-self feeling of anger and need to emerge. This feeling of anger, hate, and need does not just disappear. It incubates and seeks expression in many forms. The individual feels a vague, free-floating, emotional uncomfortableness. The child does not know why it is feeling this way. What is happening is that the defense mechanism of repressive behavior is incomplete and inefficient in stamping out the feeling of anger. It is not working. The real-self feeling is emerging…knocking on the door of consciousness from its repressed position in the unconscious. When this occurs, our child, because its unconscious exists as unconscious to it, becomes more anxious. Anxiety is really not a feeling. It is a bodily reaction to the emergence of a real feeling—anger in this story. The individual is more concerned because of the unknown nature of the discomfort. The child can't stop this discomfort. The child realizes that it has no control over its anxiety. This realization results in one of deeper disorganization. A wider gap between the self-concept's use of defense mechanisms and the emergence of the real self comes about. A snowballing effect now takes place. The more reality calls up the real self and the self-concept into existence, the more the individual fears the real-self emotion. The fear generates a defensive pattern of behavior repressing the experience of calling up the two selves. The real emotion releases itself past the inefficient guard of the defense mechanism. The perception of this appearance of the real-self emotion of anger causes more anxiety.

A change in the state of being dammed up that is caused by this conflict seems possible only if the original feeling breaks through the walls of the defense.[64]

In order not to experience this anxiety, a "heavier guard"—a stronger defense mechanism—is needed. Exaggerated and heavy defense-mechanistic behavior in an attempt to control and not experience anxiety is abnormal behavior.

Our child here is engaging in an acute inner defense struggle, becoming restless, agitated, upset, and feeling that it needs some change.[65] The difficulty is that the individual does not know what the change should be. The conflict involved becomes abnormal when our child cannot dam up the conflict anymore, when the child cannot control by any means at hand the anxiety it feels. The child is unconsciously snowballing into and pushed into a behavior pattern that it does not choose freely but must go along with if it is to survive. Our parable-story child begins to experience this.[66]

This experience issues its own symptoms: behavior that shows misevaluation of the reality situation in which the child finds itself; behavior manifesting this deep-seated conflict between the real self and the self-concept; behavior that cannot measure up to interpersonal norms because of the preceding two burdens. This experience is an attempt to frantically stop the real emotion from appearing.

Before a detailed look at the causes of this human experience, a brief description of this activity is in order as a data reservoir for our story. These manners of handling anxiety are reactions that channel the anxiety tension down some modality of human behavior. Reactions can be those of a depressive nature, those of an obsessive-compulsive nature, or phobic. General reaction categories include conversion reaction, dissociate reaction, and anxiety reaction.[67] The key to this enumeration is the word "reaction." The reactive pattern of experience might appear as a symptom involving bodily faculties.[68] The place where the symptom appears is not as important as the reason behind the appearance of the pattern. The important insight here is that a symptom is an expression and nothing more. The reaction habit or pattern of behavior, no matter how manifested, is only that, a behavior pattern, a symptom of some internal unresolved conflict and pain.[69]

Underlying the basic release patterns are general dispositions that a person suffering this manifests. Generally the individual is unable to handle stress situations of any type. Our traveler toward God is involved in his or her own inadequacies, fears, and emotional life, is generally tense and jumpy, and continually feels disjointed or incongruent. This results in an overall feeling of unhappiness, dissatisfaction, and incompleteness. This is a list of symptoms...of reactions...of ways for the self-concept to convert the anxiety felt into its own acceptable form.

How has such suffering developed? Considering, as I have throughout this narrative description, the emotional causes, I would have to say that the primary cause is the inability to handle the anger the child feels toward its mother for not providing unconditional love, which is its birthright.[70] This inability generally occurs because development isn't sophisticated enough at the time of the appearance of this experience of rejection for a child to handle it. The influx of rejection is simply too difficult for a defenseless child to stabilize. The child has to settle for as much of its goal of "trusted"-"truster" as it can. Maybe it would only be 20 percent. The child is very needy. A barrier stands between the self and the need for love; the barrier is the unfulfilling and rejecting significant other, the person's mother. The goal is that the real self may emerge to meet reality as a truster perfectly at home and in harmony with its self-concept, what one thinks about oneself and the world. But as is seen, this did not happen. Instead a very painful experience began, a condition of idealized emotional-conceptual growth leaving behind the real self because the real self was angry and in deep pain. The child is one who justly and truthfully has hostile feelings for the person whose life it needs.[71] In our descriptive vignette, as the self-concept establishing continued, it took upon itself the character of "perfection." Its assumptions about itself and reality always "had to be something."[72] The self-concept never could relax on the real self. The self-concept is built on theoretical assumptions having no ground in the child's real self. It is an unreal self-concept that is forming. This is the individual's frame of reference (self-concept): "I have to be good"; "I must be the best." This is an expression of Karen Horney's "search for glory." The emotional perception of the growing separation between one's real self and one's assumptions of oneself, one's self-concept, begins to create a tension. This tension is concretized when reality calls the child to work from one frame of reference as reality would innocently do. The child immediately acts out of its "theoretical construct," its self-concept.

Because our traveler has at the real-self level the emotion of anger and rage, the individual feels that somehow he or she is "bad." This feeling the child has is magnified by what it learns: "Mommy and Daddy are great people; everyone loves them;" "All good children love their parents." The child's self-concept immediately latches on to this as an assumption because the child "must be good." What happens is that the self-concept is growing in one direction, the assumption of "How good I am because of the degree to which I love my parents," while the real self develops in another direction and incubates the just anger and rage that exists for the parents. This is a conflicting and opposing development.[73] A child feels very guilty and "bad" for feeling this anger and rage for its parents. "The human being which they actually are keeps interfering significantly with their flight to glory and, therefore, they are bound to hate it, to hate themselves."[74]

What happens? The child suppresses this.[75] But reality continually calls both selves to the fore. The next attempt at handling this situation is to stop the "call": don't contact reality! This is a defense mechanism. As emotional energy dwindles, the defenses drop, and as these defending behaviors relax, the broadening real emotion perceives the self-conceptual realm of activity. More emotional energy is needed to dam up this feeling; a habitual reaction sets in as the person becomes a plaything between the conflicting impulses of the two selves. "The reaction is brought about when this conflict generates anxiety and the attempts to allay anxiety lead in turn to defensive tendencies."[76]

Our narrative description about emotional suffering has not been an all-inclusive one developing all psychological causes involved in the formation of the many and variant reaction habits. It has been an attempt to indicate and describe the suffering in a typical way. This follows classical psychological categories for the purpose of showing interior emotional development and suffering.

Discussion Questions

In order not to experience within themselves the pain of loss, the loss of a parent's love and trust, people repress their inner being and repress outside reality. This is a bad habit. Does God want this changed? Why?

Does God want you to be the self God created you to be? Why?

Does God want you to be free from a way of thinking about yourself that is not true? Why?

Escaping from inner pain does not resolve or heal it. Does God want this pain healed? How does God bring this about?

When is repression a bad habit?

Fear of one's real-self feeling generates the bad habit of defensive repression. Discuss.

CHAPTER FIVE

The Dark Night of Anxiety

If this state of emotional conflict continues in an unattended and unexamined way for an extended period of time, the feeling of guilt for experiencing deep-seated anger, hate, and aggression will become unconscious and then show itself as an undifferentiated, free-floating anxiety.[77] The individual involved in this dynamic makes statements such as these upon seeking relief: "I don't know what's wrong. I just feel bad"; "I feel something's wrong"; "I feel uncomfortable but I can't get at it." The dammed-up state of the individual's basic emotional conflict has caused a twofold block. First of all, emotional responses are repressed; second, no emotional warmth, affection, support, or love can enter. Our traveler toward God has basic human needs for love, tenderness, trust, and esteem that must be met. These are not being met because in repressing one emotional state the individual has inadvertently and unconsciously suppressed the ability to receive any effective stimuli or to emote with any affective response. Our traveler is now emotionally starving to death. This starving to death, this suffering, is translated to the traveler under the guise of feelings of guilt, shame, and inferiority. Suffering hits this person in feelings of guilt. Guilt is the affective state that results as a special form of anxiety or tension when one violates some principle or some condition of one's own human existence.[78] Guilt is a warning signal that either boundaries have been transgressed or the establishment of new self boundaries must take place, as otherwise the self will be weakened and possibly destroyed by the resulting loss of self-respect and self-identity. Why and how does this occur? This question can be answered by finding out just what principles in our pilgrim's consciousness or unconsciousness are being violated or transgressed. It can be seen from chapter 3 that our traveler is involved in an idealized self-concept formation that consists of incorrect child ideas, conclusions, assumptions, and resultant feelings about who the self is.

According to Karen Horney, the child then looks to other places, not itself, in forming ideas about itself. This child is unable to dip into its real self for resources and information, so it dips into others'—into who others are, into who others want to be, and into who others want the child to be. Our traveler delegates or farms out his or her emotional responsibility to others, giving this power over self to others. The person becomes "outer directed."[79] This, however, is not outside the child. The child has internalized all of these outer-directed goals or "ways to be." They are a set of shoulds or musts within the child, and they act as its own self-concept, its resource and fund of action.[80] These "ways to be" that the child internalizes as its self-concept are the principles that the child violates and transgresses as it attempts, consciously or unconsciously, to be itself, its real self. When this occurs, our traveler feels guilty.[81] "If guilt feelings are carefully examined and are tested for genuineness, it becomes apparent that much of what looks like feelings of guilt is the expression either of anxiety or of a defense against it."[82] The child says emotionally, "I have done something either wrong or against myself."

The child also experiences an affective state when it cannot live up to its "way to be." This is the feeling of shame...a not doing "something that I could have" or a not doing "something that I should have been able to do."[83] Suffering hits our pilgrim now in feelings of shame. This can become an all-pervading affective state as one's idealized self-concept formation is fundamentally out of reach of one's real self and, consequently, impossible for the child to live up to.

As our traveler develops and grows up with this conflict unresolved, he or she will, by necessity, change his or her environment from parents and the home situation to a more peer-group-oriented lifestyle. Since our child's self-concept has had to rely so heavily on others for strength, this will continue; the individual's "outer direction" will not so much come from parents but from "equals"... peers. At this point in our traveler's development, the personality of the difficulty changes. The cognitive label one initially pins on his or her undifferentiated anxiety takes on a new context. Peer-group "ways to be" become one's own "ways to be." However, this is not satisfactory to a young person. Our pilgrim cannot seem to function well enough. Something seems to be wrong "even in this situation." Our young person is not able to successfully be "the way" he or she thinks the peer group is and wants one to be. The individual's own unresolved conflict of two selves rushing to meet reality has taken up so much energy that one can't "keep up," usually socially, with peers. The resultant feeling, according to Alfred Adler, is one of inferiority. Suffering now hits our traveler with feelings of inferiority. "I'm no good...I can't perform the way they do." This is the root area of the formation of an inferiority complex. The complex, however, is predictable and, really, a further outgrowth of the same emotional dynamic that originally gave rise to a pervasive and painful feeling of guilt, then shame, and now inferiority.

> Guilt feelings, like inferiority feelings, are not at all unwelcome; the neurotic person is far from eager to get rid of them. In fact he insists on his guilt and vigorously resists every attempt to exonerate him. This attitude alone would suffice to indicate that behind his insistence on feeling guilty there must, as in inferiority feelings, be a tendency which is an important function.[84]

Because of the fundamental ground of our pilgrim's idealized self-concept—outside the real self—his or her roots cannot be nourished. They hang "out somewhere" where none of the water or rich earth of the real self can fortify them. The pilgrim does not stand upon the rock of his or her self in strength and so withers.

The real self rebels against the self-concept; the result is to suffer feelings of guilt. The real self cannot measure up to the demands of the self-concept internalized from the parents; the result is to suffer feelings of shame. Our pilgrim's real self cannot live up to the self-concept feeding off the expectations of others; the result is to suffer feelings of inferiority.[85]

Guilt is vague. Shame is a vague feeling. Inferiority is a difficult feeling to get at. The reason for this is that these feelings are only symptomatic of the real problem...the basic unresolved emotional conflict, which, because left unexamined, has become repressed and unconscious.[86] What is conscious? The feelings...the suffering...of guilt, shame, and inferiority. The three cognitive labels used here are an attempt to deal with an ever present feeling of anxiety...an anxiety resulting from the fact that the real self does not have free and unhampered access to reality and vice versa.[87] Why is the idealized self-concept here so rigid and tenacious, so durable and resilient, so complete and observant? The idealized self-concept has developed through pushing off and away from the real self because the real self is in such pain. The projected self-concept is formed basically as an accumulation of what the person wants to be, not who he or she is. Our traveler feels angry...feels like a hater. Our traveler does not like feeling that and so sets up for the self a goal that will constitute extreme aggrandizement and honor, which the traveler feels will furnish the self-esteem that he or she feels so desperately in need of.[88]

Internal statements such as these appear as this dynamic realizes itself: "I am enraged"; "Nobody likes an angry enraged hater...especially one who feels this way toward their parents"; "I want to be loved and to love. I feel I am unlovable because it is my fault that my parents don't love me. I'll become 'this' or I'll become 'that' and then people will love me." Usually the "this" or the "that" is some career or role that the person perceives society to value. It embodies all of the qualities that the enraged angry person feels not to have. The angry person feels that if one realizes this, one will feel good about oneself. This, of course, goes on in complete blindness to the fact that maybe the real self of the young person has potentially all of these qualities anyway.

> Probably the worst drawback is the ensuing alienation from the self. We cannot suppress or eliminate essential parts of ourselves without becoming estranged from ourselves. It is one of those changes gradually produced by neurotic processes that despite their fundamental nature come about unobserved. The person simply becomes oblivious to what he really feels, likes, rejects, believes, in short, to what he really is. Without knowing it he may live the life of his image.[89]

Without taking cognizance of the real self, the setting of "who one wants to be emotionally" establishes itself as the self-concept: the person one needs to think one is. In this self-concept hope is not entirely future-orientated. It admits of the traveler's foreknowledge and intuitive sense of being aware of love as a human reality. The goal of the self-concept is the key to the development of many habitual emotional states, personality characteristics, and abnormal emotional conditions. Personality characteristics and emotional states now form as clothes of the hoped-for goal: "that certain effect" which is the project being striven for.

The basic feeling of anger effects a state of emergency in our traveler's emotional organism: aggression, a compulsive reaction of wanting to escape the feeling of insecurity and inferiority by leaping out of one's emotional skin. Our pilgrim sets out to be superior...to strive to overcome inferior feelings. This is a self-imposed pressure.[90] It is directed at all of the capabilities and talents a person has. Our pilgrim demands excessive success from himself or herself and his or her talents, strangling every bit of success out of them to prove to the self that one is a good person. Our traveler does not have a gentle hold on his or her self, capabilities, and development. Our pilgrim does not water the developing plant of his or her capabilities with care, warm sunlight, and patient encouragement. Instead the individual violently demands immediate success and intimate perfection from his or her self and all talents and capabilities.[91]

Common language would put it this way: "They are very hard on themselves." This dynamic emanates from the incessant fear that loss of the habitual emotional pattern of demanding ultimate perfection of oneself would leave the person with nothing. This fear of nothingness is actually a cloak covering the original crippling sense of inferiority and inadequacy at feeling anger. For our pilgrim, this need for aggressive overcompensating through excessive goal achievement now becomes the way to feel good about oneself.

> The need for vindictive triumph as an antidote to feeling humiliated may be acted upon or may exist mainly in the neurotic's own mind; it may be conscious or unconscious, but it is one of the driving forces in the neurotic's need for superiority and gives it its special coloring.[92]

Everything now falls into place. All is now developed and folded into our traveler's personality in terms of its usefulness or value in contributing to this end.

Discussion Questions

Do you think that if you repress one emotion, you inadvertently repress all of your emotions? Why?

What does it mean to be outer directed?

Is being outer directed a bad habit? Discuss in your group.

Does God want your ideas, conclusions, assumptions, and feelings about yourself to be based in the perception of your real self?

Does God want you to be able to go to your own internal experiences for information about yourself?

Does God want an adult to be outer directed?

What is the unconscious?

Does God want human beings to be oblivious to what they feel?

Is living by a false image of one's self a bad habit?

How deep are bad habits? What causes them? How are they constructed and built and maintained?

CHAPTER SIX

The Dark Night of Inaccuracy

The thought and experience of Alfred Adler, a Vienna-born psychiatrist and early coworker with Sigmund Freud, can be of assistance to us in this story-parable. The term "inferiority complex" was first used in association with the developments Adler made in his *Individual Psychology*...a new creative viewpoint caused by both conflict with and reaction to the thought and insights of Sigmund Freud.[93] A correct understanding of the Adlerian theory of "inferiority feelings" will be necessary as an essential building block in taking a look at the human emotional suffering in the life of the traveler in our descriptive narrative.

According to Alfred Adler's theory, suffering hits our traveler in terms of feelings of inferiority that may be masked as superiority.[94] Adler, in taking up this investigation, found that there was a basic feeling of inferiority that is natural to all human beings.[95] We find ourselves in the environment of our world as small, weak, and positively completely helpless...as babies. We simply are inferior to other human beings in our environment as regards strength, sensory-motor ability, and development in every area of human potential. A true perception on a child's part would issue therefore in a natural feeling of inferiority.

A child finds itself depending upon its environment. If a child is unwanted, if it is hated, if it is rejected, it will make an emotional decision concerning its ability to cope with this experience. Our child's decision runs along these lines: "I can cope with this!" or "I can't cope with this unless I..." If the child has defective health, is diseased, or is dysfunctional physically, it will be faced with the same emotional decision.[96] Adler also brings in another environmental condition that, when present, elicits the same necessary decision from a child: the condition of pampering. Pampering is a process of isolation. Pampering is isolating a child from experience and reality contact by simply protecting the child from reality contact or removing the child from such contact. Pampering is a process of lavishing affection and attention upon a child to the exclusion of any other reality contact.[97] The result in a child would be a receptive-passive emotional posture waiting for the influx of positive feedback.

> Whenever a mother abounds too evidently with excessive affection and makes behavior, thought, and action, and even speech, superfluous for the child, then the child will be more readily inclined to develop as a parasite exploiter, and look to other persons for everything he wants....He will display egotistic tendencies and regard it as his right to suppress people and to be always pampered by them.[98]

The decision our pilgrim is faced with at this point is the same as the above, but its development is more sophisticated. This young traveler, inundated with rejection and anger, cannot be completely safeguarded from stress contact. Upon this stress contact, the child immediately asks the question of itself "Can I cope?" The response is either "I can cope" or "I can't cope unless I..." The response decision involves an alternative avenue: "I can't cope unless I do something." This is generally something along the lines of "SUCCEED...GET ON TOP OF IT."[99] Here our pilgrim reacts violently to the particularly increased inferiority feeling and says, "I'll never let myself get into a position like this again." This is a deep emotional decision that mobilizes our traveler's emotional, intellectual, and personal talent in a striving posture."[100] The "readiness" or the striving posture of any potential is an attempt to cope with the feelings our traveler feels inside the self. These feelings have an object outside the child...in reality. This mobilization, then, is not to cope with reality but to cope with the feelings of our child traveler toward reality, the world outside the child. This is a fundamental mistake and fundamentally inaccurate, as our pilgrim has the total mechanism with which to cope with reality but instead mobilizes all energies to cope with reality via an indirect method...a sort of striving and building up of one's own castle "higher than yours"...or reality's.[101] Our traveler sets out to build a castle so high over against reality (the threatening reality being encountered) that the "other" will be dwarfed and, "seeing the greatness" of the child, will marvel and cower in the presence of the great castle constructed by our young person. The result is that the threatening reality of the other will then move away beaten and destroyed, all without our traveler actually directly expressing his or her feeling to the other. Our young traveler is successful, has coped with this threat and has been victorious. It is to be noted here again that this is a fundamental mistake and fundamentally inaccurate on the part of the child. There is no direct communication of feeling, such as, "I'm angry at you because you said this or that, or did this or that." The expression of feeling is an indirect expression. It is a mode of proceeding that carries the weight of the feeling without actually delivering it to whom it belongs in reality. This is the problem: the enormous energy needed to maintain this posture of striving for superiority over the environment as an attempt to express the feeling of hostility. The energy needed is very great.[102] The emotional energy necessary to mobilize all of one's powers and abilities drags upon one's personal supply of psychic strength. This drain on our traveler is coupled with the continued frustration of not expressing the feeling of hostility because it falls short, having chosen an indirect method of expression. The results and meaning of this condition will form the problem addressed in the latter section of this chapter.

Adler here enters with his own theory of what has taken place. He says what has taken place was the formation of a "style of life." The "style of life" for Adler is a general concept comprising the personal goal of a person, the individual's opinion of self and the world and a unique way of striving for his or her goal in the particular circumstances.[103] In our example, our traveler's personal goal was to be superior to everyone in all circumstances. Our pilgrim's opinion of self is that he or she cannot cope with reality without continuing to "strive, strive, strive" for perfection. Our pilgrim's opinion of the world is that the world is a competitor, something or someone to be overcome or to be forced to give love to the child. Our pilgrim's unique way of striving for his or her goal involves the unique talents and abilities he or she has. Here is the beginning of a habit...a repetitive habit.

Adler now posits as another reality observable in the formation of our individual child's psychological lifestyle the existence of a creative power in the individual.[104] Adler maintains that a person creatively reacts to stimuli, fashioning his or her own emotional lifestyle. Adler theorizes that we can understand symptom selection only if we regard it as a piece of art. We must refrain from making judgments and can only examine how every human being is an artist on life's road. Here, then, our pilgrim mysteriously selects the talents and powers that he or she believes will result in achievement of the envisaged goal of superiority over one's threatening environment.[105]

This creativity in selecting emotional styles of life can be also unveiled insofar as the depth of the impression made upon the child does not depend on the objective fact or circumstances but depends rather on how the child regards the fact or circumstances. This can be seen when two siblings are exposed to the exact same fact or circumstances. Each may react in an entirely different manner.[106]

This emotional style of life now molds and shapes all stimuli...all influences upon our pilgrim. A habit sets in. This is why Adler calls his psychology individual psychology. A person's behavior and habits spring from one's opinion of oneself. In his theory Adler calls the perceptual framework that edits reality a *schema of apperception*. The schema of apperception edits reality, and experiences are interpreted before they are accepted. The interpretation always accords with the original meaning given to life. Even if this meaning is very gravely mistaken, if the approach to our problems and tasks brings us continually into misfortunes and agonies, it is never easily relinquished. It is a habit. One's opinion of oneself and reality is, then, *active:* it does something for oneself...it is an active agent. One's schema of apperception, then—a defense—is an active emotional instrument. It is active as every psychological defense is active insofar as it is censoring material coming up into one's field of perception.[107] For our pilgrim it is a bad habit.

It is shielding, excluding, selecting, and including material continuously in accord with one's perception of self and the world. The situation a human being is in is commonly called "the world" or "life." One finds as one lives that "life," that "the world," has its own dynamic, its own direction, its own needs, its own demands, and, in general, its own tasks. One finds oneself having to "meet the tasks of life"...the "demands of the world." Freud posited the two basic tasks of life to be, one, that of work and, two, that of love.

Adler expands on that by adding to occupation and love that of friendship.[108] Adler observes this confrontation of a human person and "life." He observes that those who were successful were those who were able to live life with a measure of resolution, meeting their needs for love, work, and friendship...and that those who were "failures" were not. In his study of those who were unable to meet the tasks of life, Adler found a consistent lack of a quality he has come to call "social interest."[109] In his work he found a considerable lack of social interest to be a common denominator among those failing to function amid the tasks and demands of life. In his theory Adler then proceeds to posit the necessity of the human phenomenon of social interest in the human personality in order to meet the tasks and demands of life. Social interest is essentially to have an affective perception and readiness and concern for the feelings, the situation, the needs, and the hopes of another human being besides oneself. What occupies one's energy, personal and human, is, then, 50 percent one's own progress toward meeting one's own needs and interests and 50 percent meeting the needs and interests of another person or persons besides oneself.[110] Social interest is a certain feeling where one finds that one is at home in the human race, that one is at home on the earth and feels that another...others'...flesh is one's own flesh. What one does for another one does for oneself. It is a feeling of belongingness.

Adler uses the German word *gemeinschaftsgefühl* to describe this quality. The following terms have been used as English equivalents: social feeling, community feeling, fellow feeling, sense of solidarity, communal intuition, community interest, social sense, and social interest. Adler posits social interest as a personality barometer. He considers social interest to be an innate human potential, that is, that every human being is born with the potential of social interest and feeling. Each person is entrusted with the task of developing this quality and ability for his or her own life.[111] In his theory Adler is saying that suffering hits a person in terms of feelings of inferiority. Adler would maintain and say to our traveler that all of the attempts that our traveler would make by mobilizing his or her self to be superior in order to destroy this ever-present feeling of inferiority are a painful reaction to the nonreal self relating to the world, and insofar as this is operating, such a quest will not work for our pilgrim in bringing the desired love and hoped-for resolution.

Discussion Questions

The nature of a child is one of being dependent. Is the deep emotional decision within a child of "I will never allow myself to be in this position again" the birth of a bad habit? Why?

Is an indirect method to cope with reality a bad habit? Discuss.

Is an indirect method of emotional expression an energy drain on a person? Discuss.

How is a defense mechanism really an active agent?

How is the mistake of an inaccurate self-concept a dark night? Discuss.

Does God want bad habits changed to good habits?

Is the indirect expression of feeling a bad habit?

Your style of life is your opinion of yourself and of the world, your personal goals, and your unique way of striving for your goals in your particular circumstances. Does God have any interest in this formation in you?

The spiritual life encompasses the changing of bad habits to good habits. Discuss.

CHAPTER SEVEN

Self-Knowledge

How does our traveler move from this painful emotional experience to feeling the freedom to be his or her real self in the world? What is the process involved in this movement?

The problem can be stated that because of early traumatizing anger our pilgrim's real self-concept formation has become distorted. This results in a painful reactional relationship toward reality consisting of the real self warring with the acquired idealized self-concept to respond to any given reality stimulus. Because of the ensuing personality disorganization, the developmental needs of basic trust, autonomy, initiative, creativity, identity, and intimacy cannot be met and have not been met.[112] This bad habit results in a great deal of emotional pain.

What is needed, then, is to release the real self of our traveler to make its own way toward the realization of the developmental needs as yet unmet.[113] As Karen Horney puts it:

> The task of therapy, therefore, is to make the person aware of their idealized image in all its detail, to assist them in gradually understanding all its functions and subjective values, and to show them the suffering that it inevitably entails. They will then start to wonder whether the price is not too high. But they can relinquish the image only when the needs that have created it are considerably diminished.[114]

> The end is to help the person to regain their spontaneity, to find their measurements of value in their self, in short, to give the person the courage to be themselves.[115]

Karen Horney presents the notion of the process of moving from suffering to freedom—of moving from idealized self-concept living to real-self living—as an active one. Her notion begins with the counselor-guide's unreserved attention focused in on our traveler and what the latter is saying. The counselor-guide uses the technique of free association, having the traveler respond freely with whatever comes into his or her mind on a given subject presented by the counselor-guide.

This process "is directed toward the two available sources of information: first, what the person says about their relations with others both in the past and in the present and about their attitude toward themselves...secondly, all the peculiar drives and reactions which the person acts out inadvertently in the analytical situation itself."[116]

As our traveler is speaking, the counselor-guide has constantly in mind the question: "Why does this particular memory, thought, feeling, fantasy, or dream come up just now?"[117]

In order to uncover the unconscious process and workings of an idealized self-concept, the counselor-guide looks for clues— changes in mood...what the person omits...contradictions in the person's accounts of experiences. The counselor-guide gathers data, giving his or her own interpretation of what the meaning of the data is. The counselor-guide points out to our traveler the connections between the latter's emotional conflicts and present complaints.[118] The counselor-guide is actively driving for intellectual understanding and clarity in his or her own mind, then directly relating observations to the suffering pilgrim. The counselor-guide makes and gives tentative views and interpretations of our traveler's pain and conflicts.

Our pilgrim reacts to the interpretations of the counselor-guide, and from the fund of the former's reactions the counselor-guide can proceed. The goal of the direct interpretations of the guide is change in our suffering pilgrim from idealized false self-concept living to real-self living. The guide discusses with our traveler the latter's reactions to the guide's interpretations. The understanding from such free discussion plus the guide's attitude toward our pilgrim—one of "blind optimism" that the real self of the person can handle and overcome idealized false self-concept living—allows the traveler to understand and decide for real-self living.[119] "The guide's belief in and clear recognition of the person's potentialities helps them regain their faith in themselves."[120]

Our traveler is suffering, faced with a painful inability to allow the real self to be, and to represent the self as the self. It has been so long since the individual has done this that the real self is an unknown. Our traveler fears the unknown: the real self.[121]

> The neurotic has felt guilt as their real self has contradicted their idealized self image. They have felt shame at not being able to "live up" to their idealized image. They have felt inferiority...all painful suffering for the person.[122]

By becoming aware of one's real-self messages, one can eventually take responsibility for them and let them be...allowing the pattern of one's own real needs to resolve themselves in one's environment. After this has come into awareness, our traveler can begin to observe who their real self is...right before his or her very eyes.

> And it is only then that one recognizes one's confusion in the matter of ideals and that this begins to strike the person as undesirable. Before, the whole subject was beyond one's understanding and interest..., now for the first time one realizes that ideals have some meaning, and wants to discover what one's own ideals really are.[123]

The real self will then take charge and organize the personality of our traveler. As this takes place, emotionally painful unreal-self action and reaction evanesce, feelings of guilt, shame, and inferiority evanesce. These are supplanted by real-self need and gratification. The real self replaces the false-counterfeit-constructed idealized self-concept dynamic. Change occurs. Previous energy that was used in idealized self-concept actualization, now not needed, can be drawn upon to actualize the real-self phenomenal field.

The movement from "outer-directedness" to "inner-directedness" is the movement from false self-concept to real-self living. The early traumatic anger and hate experience of our traveler caused alienation from real feelings. The real self was not acceptable because our traveler felt that, if expressed, it would have meant that his or her safety and life support system—the parents—might abandon the traveler. The child's need is survival. Our traveler perceived that, emotionally, it was less expensive to suppress real feelings than to express them. This became so ingrained and encrusted over the years as to become unrecognizable.

Once the real self is conscious, our pilgrim can allow himself or herself to be, can allow the real self to represent him or her in reality. Our traveler can be comfortable and enjoy who he or she is.

The counselor-guide is very active in this process, observing, examining, interpreting, exploring, and questioning the course of this journey and helping, suggesting, and encouraging. "By means of these activities the counselor-guide assists the process."[124] The counselor-guide is actively using expertise, seeing and understanding how our traveler has formed and developed an idealized false concept and how the real self has been hidden and is in prison. The counselor-guide sees and understands this and interprets it to our traveler, who changes and grows until he or she can rely on his or her own real self to do the job. Our sojourner comes to real-self living…spiritual health.

Alfred Adler looks upon our traveler and the meaning of his or her emotional health and therapeutic resolution in a way that supports, deepens, and amplifies what has been presented. As was touched upon in the previous chapter, Adler sees a person to be emotionally healthy when the person is as interested in the lives of other human beings as in his or her own life. This is social interest. Adler sees psychologically healthy persons as those who are working and creating what they find the most interesting and helpful to themselves and most helpful to the human race as a whole.[125] He posits that such persons are psychologically healthy because they choose what they want to do not only in terms of their own interests but also in terms of the interests of others and, eventually, the whole human family. Psychologically healthy persons also are fed by a successful life of love and friendship. The success of their life of love has its origin in the authentic concern of psychologically healthy persons that their loved ones' needs and interests be met…and by them. Psychologically healthy persons have friends. Their consciousness that others' interests and needs constitute their own interests and needs has issued in a feeling of closeness, understanding, and familiarity with many individuals on many levels over many human interests.[126]

Seeing the problem of emotional suffering in terms of the Adlerian insight can shed some new light upon our consideration. The question can, then, be posed: How can our pilgrim move from the state of suffering mass inferiority feelings to that of feeling worthwhile as a good person, a valuable, needed entity? What is the process involved in this movement? How does our traveler in his or her spiritual life deal with incapacitating and painful feelings and work them through to attain self-appreciation and self-esteem, self-worth? How does our spiritual traveler resolve the painful emotional conflict between feelings of inferiority and the needed feelings of self-worth? Our pilgrim's inability to solve major problems in life—problems of friendship, work, and love—brings on a need for investigation: "Why?"

"A person's active bearing can only be discovered by a correct understanding of their movement when they are confronted by the problems of life."[127] Adler submits this methodology as a means of uncovering an individual's habitual lifestyle. "The most important element in therapeutics is the disclosure of the person's system or life plan."[128] He calls his method "individual lifestyle analysis." Individual lifestyle analysis is an attempt to uncover unconscious emotional decisions that are affecting one's feeling good about oneself and one's life. It is an attempt to uncover a person's own individual lifestyle—what one's emotional goals are, one's own opinion of oneself and of the world, and one's own creative and unique way of going about striving for goals in the particular circumstances—realizing the individual's own creative power in the formation of this, and that this now is a functioning habit. Adler sees his work as one of finding out just how all of this works together to "keep the person afloat" or superior to all others.[129] Adler poses these questions in his lifestyle analysis:

What are your complaints?
What was your situation when you first noticed your complaints?
What is your situation now?
What is your occupation?
Describe your parents as to their character, and their health.
If not alive, what illness caused their death?

What was their relation to yourself?
How many brothers and sisters have you?
What is your position in the birth order?
What is their attitude toward you?
How do they get along in life?
Do they also have any illness?
Who was your father's or your mother's favorite?
What illnesses did you have in childhood and what was
    your attitude to them?
What are your earliest childhood recollections?
What do you fear the most?
What is your attitude toward the opposite sex?
What occupation would have interested you the most, if
    you only could have done it?
What recurrent dreams do you have?[130]

The design of these questions, this methodology, is to uncover two patterns: one, a picture of what is going on now, in the present—what the problems are now—and, two, a picture of what went on in the past, what the problems were then.[131] A pattern as to the present and a pattern as to the past in all probability will arise. The distillation of these two patterns is the aim of this lifestyle analysis. Adler found that the elements basic to each of these patterns are a person's habitual emotional lifestyle.

He uncovers the pattern of the present through the first four questions dealing with present realities: complaints, symptoms, situations, occupation now. Here any oversensitivity or deprivation shows itself in some failure to function at a task of life.

> When an individual passes into a new situation, their hidden character traits come out. If we could directly experiment with individuals, we could find out their state of development by putting them through new and unexpected situations...it reveals their character.[132]

A person's present-day complaints will generally stem from some unfulfilled desire that can indicate the presence of an unlearned and unexamined area of developmental need. After this present-day area emerges, the next habitual pattern can come into view in answering the next six questions. These all deal with the person's childhood. Here can emerge a habitual pattern regarding early problems, complaints, and symptoms.[133] These in their turn can produce a pattern or habit showing areas of nondevelopment in the past.

Identical elements of these two habitual patterns can be verified as bona fide problem areas by the answer to the question "What are your earliest childhood recollections?" This is probably the most important question in the emotional lifestyle analysis method. The question is posed three times, asking for the three earliest childhood recollections and memories. When our traveler lists earliest childhood recollections, Adler would note all of the details in them, especially the reactions of our traveler. The reason Adler puts such heavy emphasis on the early recollections, one's memories, is that he believes that there is a reason you remember what you do. There is a reason you select out of all of the possible memories that you have the ones that you selected. Adler posits that the reason our traveler selects certain memories is that these are the occasions, the situations, the experiences in which he or she made emotional decisions that were so deep that they constituted the beginning of his or her whole habitual psychological lifestyle.[134] It is crucially important to our traveler's current functioning lifestyle to remember these memories because they are the birthplace and the reason for the existence of his or her own individual habitual psychological style of life.

> There are no "chance memories" out of the incalculable number of impressions which meet an individual, one chooses to remember only those which one feels, however darkly, to have a bearing on one's situation. Thus one's memories represent one's "Story of My Life," a story the individual repeats to themselves...[135]

These early recollections are of major importance to our traveler's emotional lifestyle, for its establishment as well as its maintenance. This is why these memories are selected out of the vast experiences our traveler has.

As Adler mentioned, our traveler's psychological lifestyle is a work of art put together by our traveler alone. Karen Horney puts this phenomenon this way: "It represents a kind of artistic creation in which opposites appear reconciled or in which, at any rate, they no longer appear as conflicts to the individual themselves."[136]

This is the realization of self-knowledge. This self-knowledge, recognition, resolution, and integration release our traveler to live his or her real life. It also is a work of art to decipher the workings and meaning of our traveler's individual psychological lifestyle.

Those habitual unconscious elements, however, which remain constant appear in the present pattern of emotional life, in the past pattern of emotional life, and also in our traveler's earliest recollections. They constitute the emotional goals of our traveler, his or her opinion of self and world. They constitute how our traveler has formed goals and opinions and how our traveler has chosen to strive to work toward their realization. Once this is seen as a working and fully functioning unity, it can be exposed for what it is: a fairly poor way of going about meeting one's needs. The awareness that our traveler is involving his or her self in this unconscious mechanism illuminates other possibilities of action and other goals...and other means of attaining these goals. This awareness allows our traveler the possibility of choice. It allows the presence of other goals. It allows the presence of the innate potentiality of social interest. It allows our traveler the possibility of striving to enhance the interests and needs of someone outside himself or herself. This then opens the door for our traveler to have social interest as a goal in life...to act this way and then to experience living and striving not only for the self but for all humankind. Our traveler, experiencing the self feeling and acting this way, can then experience a good feeling about himself or herself, experience himself or herself as a good person...a worthwhile person...a value: this is the feeling of self-esteem, the feeling of self-worth. It is the realization of this potential in our traveler that heralds the evanescence of the feeling of inferiority and the emergence of the emotionally healthy real self. This effects the changing of bad habits to good habits.

The traveler in our parable-story here depicts and experiences what Alfred Adler and Karen Horney describe in the journey to health through therapy. Our traveler experiences deep emotional pain and starvation from spending life living from an unreal-self platform of relating to others. The result is a deep dissatisfaction and unhappiness. This emotional pain festers over years and years within our traveler, who finally "breaks down" and "breaks through" and seeks out "a guide" to express pain and deep dissatisfaction.

Our traveler erupts in pain to the guide. The traveler cannot go on living in this way. This is a breakthrough.

The real-self ache, need, rage, and sorrow have broken through the unreal-self habits of living and relating. Deep fear engulfs our pilgrim. The fear of the unknown encompasses the pilgrim, who asks, "What is my real self like?"

The real radical self is emerging and answering the question after years of repression. This is all consciously unknown to our pilgrim, who is terrorized by "the newness" of who he or she really is. Getting used to the anger, the need, the sorrow, and the love of the real self is what is at hand. As the pilgrim's guide assists by affirming the unabashed and unapologetic presence of one's real-self emotions, the traveler becomes accustomed to, and even more courageous in owning, his or her true-self vitalizing reactions. This appropriating day by day, moment by moment, experience by experience, feeling by feeling, naturally grows as our traveler recognizes when he or she is relating to others in life from the real self. As this occurs, the traveler sees ever more clearly his or her deeply engrained bad habit of false-self relating. As this movement to wholeness grows, our traveler is enabled to live life on his or her own, leaving the guide, and the journey to health begins to become a good habit.

Discussion Questions

What is the price of living a false self-concept life? Is the price too high?

What is the relationship between unresolved unconscious early childhood experiences and contemporary, here-and-now personal problems?

Does God want you to become aware of your real-self reactions? Why?

What is "social interest"?

Do you think there are no chance memories? Discuss.

Has your real self been an unknown to you? Describe your journey into your unknown real-self living. Share your journey in your group.

How does this change to real-self living occur?

Are early memories spiritual? Do they affect your spiritual life? Do they affect your bad habits? Do they affect your good habits?

Is the story of your spiritual life tied up with your memories?

Is your story one of changing bad habits to good habits?

How is this change painful? Is this change "inner pennance"?

PART THREE

Holy Weakness

CHAPTER EIGHT

Holy Weakness

As we began this consideration together, I presented to you the intent of this work on the spiritual life. I also brought up what I hoped your intent would be. My part is to present to you dimensions of the spiritual life within the origin of human emotional growth and the human mystical encounter with God. My hope is that basic patterns would be exposed and bring to light salient areas of this human experience. What is at hand for you, then, is to "find yourself" or situate yourself within these emerging dimensions. From thus situating yourself, the hoped-for balance, stability, and feeling of understanding can emerge. This resultant affective state is a conviction that your own experience is not abnormal...that where you are is understandable and historically rooted. It is a conviction that your own experience within these dimensions is in the divine arena of the spiritual life and therefore is holy. This feeling of assurance allows you, the reader, to look at and deal with your own life experience with a new vigor and dignity and conviction coming from the very meaning of holiness.

We have seen emotional struggle, pain, and suffering in chapters 3 through 7. In the next three chapters we will see the theologically equivalent experience. The term "spirituality" as I am using it from a Roman Catholic tradition encompasses the reality of how one relates to God: the "personality" of one's relationship to God and the manner in which God relates to a person. The phrase "the spirituality of Saint so-and-so" can be paraphrased as "the story of how God relates to Saint so-and-so." What God does and how God acts toward a person and the reaction a person has to God when moved by God form the very meaning of spirituality. The spirituality of a person is the story of the person's relationship to God. We will see in the next chapters the pain, struggle, and suffering in the lives of human beings consciously relating to their Creator, their God. In the following chapters we will look at saints of the church—clear examples of holiness—in order to see clearly the pattern of God's presence in their lives. Once we can clearly distill the pattern of this dynamic of God's presence, we will turn and look to see this pattern in the life and experience of our pilgrim's emotional life journey.

As a matrix for the entire investigation, I will consider what Christian spirituality has come to mean historically, by selecting spiritualities from individual human members of the church. I will be drawing upon the experience of St. Paul, St. John of the Cross, and St. Ignatius of Loyola.

Let us begin with the great apostle of Christ, Paul of Tarsus. What was his experience? How does Paul experience his humanity? What did Paul's relationship to Jesus mean to him in his life? What does Paul's spirituality mean to him? What is the spiritual life for Paul?

Paul writes, "But they will not ask his help unless they believe in him, and they will not believe in him unless they have heard of him, and they will not hear of him unless they get a preacher, and they will not have a preacher unless one is sent" (Rom 10:14). One who is "sent" is an apostle; and Paul himself refers to his own apostleship in these terms: "Paul, a servant of Christ Jesus who has been called to be an apostle, and especially chosen to preach the Good News that God promised" (Rom 1:1–2).

The subject of this consideration has a context: the above-mentioned apostleship. Paul of Tarsus is involved in a dynamic relationship with God the Father, with Jesus Christ, and with the Holy Spirit in which his response is acceptance to the impulse of God's will. This is a mystical experience and eludes the boundaries of Paul's analysis and description.[137]

God is not only the Creator of all humanity but the fulfillment of all human existence, as we will only be complete in God. God also is intimately concerned that our fulfillment come about and so offers God's own self to bring humanity to this fulfillment. Christ offers more than willing providence. Christ offers concrete direction through the Holy Spirit.

Paul is a person with a task that encompasses a twofold reality. Paul must listen attentively and carefully to the Holy Spirit and must bring this encounter message to those to whom God desires him to bring it. Paul is one sent...one sent by someone (God) to someone (the women and men of his time). He is an apostle of God.

It is in this context, then, that we proceed in an investigation of the meaning of "weakness" in the life and spirituality of Paul of Tarsus.

In writing to the Corinthians, Paul says, "For it is when I am weak that I am strong" (2 Cor 12:10). How can such a contradictory statement be true? How can a person at one and the same moment be utterly weak and massively strong, as Paul indicates his condition to be?

In considering the experience of "weakness" in Paul and then gradually doing the same with the seemingly contradictory yet concurrent reality of "strength," I hope to conclude by resolving the apparent difficulty. Paul's condition of weakness means his absolute feebleness and impotence in effecting any qualitative change in a given situation.[138] Within the context of the life of Paul, this weakness, a quality of Paul's own being, must be related to, and identified with, Jesus Christ. For Jesus Christ is everything for Paul: "I believe nothing can happen that will outweigh the supreme advantage of knowing Christ Jesus my Lord....I look on everything as so much rubbish if only I can have Christ" (Phil 3:8–10).

Paul is a person whose entire being and meaning is union with Jesus Christ. This is who Paul is: union with Jesus Christ.[139] From this fullness Paul can exhort the Ephesians,

> Out of God's infinite glory, may God give you the power through his Spirit for your hidden selves to grow strong, so that Christ may live in your hearts through faith, and then, planted in love and built in love you will with all the saints have strength to grasp the breadth and length, the height and the depth; until knowing the love of Christ, which is beyond all knowledge, you are filled with the utter fullness of God. (Eph 3:16–19)

Paul's union with Jesus Christ, this fullness of which he speaks, is Paul's strength. "There is nothing I cannot master with the help of the one who gives me strength" (Phil 4:13). It is because Paul is one with Jesus Christ that he can do and speak of the things he does.

What is the meaning of weakness in Paul's life and spirituality? Weakness is Paul's awareness that he can do nothing by himself. This awareness is born out of his experience of suffering:

> I have been sent to prison more often and whipped so many times more, often almost to death. Five times I had the thirty-nine lashes from the Jews; three times I have been beaten with sticks; once I was stoned; three times I have been shipwrecked and once adrift in the open sea for a night and a day...in danger from rivers and in danger from brigands...I have been hungry and thirsty and often starving; I have been in the cold without clothes. (2 Cor 11:23–29)

Also in 2 Corinthians 12:7 Paul mentions a "thorn of the flesh" that was given to him by God. What is the relationship here between the sufferings, trials, and obstacles that Paul is faced with and his weakness? These trials Paul is faced with exact from him all of his emotional, physical, and personal energy. A state of mental, emotional, and physical exhaustion ensues. At this moment Paul is faced with his condition: his inability to contribute any energy from any one of his faculties in attempting to remedy his situation, his inability to effect any qualitative change in the situation he is facing. This is the "feebleness" Paul talks about in Second Corinthians. This recognition involves the apprehension by Paul that he, in this condition, cannot be the source of any more energy or creative power. This speaks, to some degree, of Paul's state of weakness.

What is God doing during these experiences? How is the One who is Paul's everything involved in these experiences? God is involved as Paul is disarmed, bit by bit and little by little, of every source of energy and life that Paul is accustomed to draw on. Every person or situational comfort or help that Paul would be accustomed to summon up as a source of life has become nonfunctional. The sufferings of Paul cast him into the condition of relying on his own abilities and capacities, on himself. Paul's sufferings drain these abilities and capacities of all existing energy and power. Paul is more than alone; he is burdened "often almost to death" (2 Cor 11:24). He is weak.

At this moment within the experience of Paul, when Paul is devoid of energy, Jesus Christ reveals his presence to Paul—within him..."fulfilling" him...fulfilling the vacuum...filling the void... giving life and pulling him through an impossible situation. As Paul speaks in exhorting Timothy:

> The first time I had to present my defense, there was not a single witness to support me. Every one of them deserted me—may they not be held accountable for it. But the Lord stood by me and gave me power, so that through me the whole message might be proclaimed for all the pagans to hear; and so l was rescued from the lion's mouth. The Lord will rescue me from all evil attempts on me, and bring me safely to his heavenly kingdom. (2 Tim 4:16–18)

This experience is very vivid for Paul. The sensibility is understandable. Paul, conscious of his state of weakness, can apprehend and sense immediately any motion of God within him. Any movement of God, the source of life and energy, is going to be obvious as "Other" over against the void of exhaustion.[140] The vividness of this experience yields a perceptible joy and thanksgiving: "Blessed be God and Father of our Lord Jesus Christ, a gentle Father and God of all consolation, who comforts us in all our sorrows" (2 Cor 1:3–4). This vivid meeting with God—a meeting and a presence that cannot be mistaken for anyone but God—is Paul's most valued experience. Paul's everything is God Himself, and Paul's encounters with his everything are reverenced as such.

Paul boasts of this weakness. He welcomes the experience of his own weakness. Paul rejoices in his own weakness and goes even further:

> So I shall be very happy to make my weakness my special boast so that the power of Christ may stay over me, and that is why I am quite content with my weakness, and with

insults, hardships, persecutions, and the agonies I go through for Christ's sake. (2 Cor 1 2:9, 10)

Paul values the experience of his own weakness so highly not because of his own inner exhaustion but because of the presence of the God and Father of Jesus Christ and the presence of Jesus himself, which comfort him in his weakness.[141] It is his state of weakness—the utter inability of Paul to tap the energy sources he normally would draw on and the inability to generate any more creative energy from his own capacities—that issues itself in a cry of absolute need to God.[142] Because this cry of Paul is answered, he can say, "For it is when I am weak that I am strong" (2 Cor 12:10). Is this a contradictory statement? Is this a statement of Paul's weakness? Or is this a statement of Paul's holiness and strength in God? It is only in the power of God that Paul is strong, and Paul values this presence of power.[143] For Paul the power of God is most obvious during his moments of weakness. Paul experiences God saying, "My grace is enough for you: my power is at its best in weakness" (2 Cor 12:9). Paul rejoices in this. If this is when God's power is at its best in him, Paul invites it and is content with this.[144] Paul therefore sees his experience of weakness as being his most precious state, for then the God of his life comes. Then is Paul strong, "for if God is with me who is against me." This, then, is not a contradictory statement; it is not a statement of weakness. It is, in actuality, a statement of Paul's holiness and strength.

What have these experiences of suffering, trials, persecutions, and troubles—this weakness—taught Paul? The cumulative effect of all of these experiences on Paul in his apostolate has been that Paul sees God as the source of his being, that he drinks continually at this source. Because of this recognition and experience, Paul says, "Because it is by grace that you have been saved, through faith; not by anything of your own, but by a gift from God; not by anything that you have done, so that nobody can claim the credit. We are God's work of art" (Eph 2:8–9).

Paul apprehends God as totally Other because of his previous experience of vacuum. From this experience he can easily see that the nature of his holiness and strength and success is a gift from this Other. "Paul himself was conscious of remaining, not only in this state of weakness, but also in the state of complete giving of himself to Christ; and it was by this gift that he became all things to all."[145]

The vividness of this is the ground of Paul's proclamation to the Christians, Jews, and Gentiles.[146] Paul is an apostle: one sent by God to the women and men of his times. The content of the message that Paul speaks to these women and men is the content of his experience of God.[147] What will Paul preach? What will he say? He can only preach of his relationship to God and how this relationship originated, deepens, and grows in his experience of his own weakness. So it is Paul's weakness that allows the Spirit to act so freely in him. This, then, is the source of the holiness and the strength of his fellow sisters and brothers; for "they will not ask his help unless they believe in him" (Rom 10:14). And unless Paul preaches to them about Jesus, they will not cry out to him in their weakness and consequently will not believe and be saved. Paul can say, then, "We are glad to be weak provided you are strong" (2 Cor 13:9). And again, "When we are made to suffer, it is for your consolation and salvation" (2 Cor 1:6).

This experience of holiness turns Paul to the future and to coming difficulties with hope, courage, and confidence:[148]

Not to rely on ourselves but on God, who raises the dead to life….God will save us again; yes that is our firm hope in God, that in the future God will save us again….So I shall be very happy to make my weakness my special boast. (2 Cor 1:9–10; 12:9)

It is this experience of holiness that bridges his former life ("Meanwhile Saul was still breathing threats to slaughter the Lord's disciples" [Acts 9:1]) and his present one ("You might have thousands of guardians in Christ, but not more than one father and it was I who begot you in Christ Jesus by preaching the Good News" [1 Cor 4:15, 16]). Paul's former self has passed away and his "hidden self" (Eph 3:16) has grown strong. He now speaks of love and holiness and not war. He is patient and loving and not vengeful and murderous.

His encounter with Jesus Christ and his ensuing experience of weakness to strength in his Lord Jesus have reached deep into Paul's life, freeing his capacity to love, to nurture others, and to care for them and their welfare in the Lord—to be holy. Paul is now a "new creation" (2 Cor 5:17) "planted deep in love and built on love" (Eph 3:18). Paul, indeed, is a changed person. He is a person of deep freedom and love.

In Philippians 3:20–21 Paul delves into the mystery that has possessed him: "The Lord Jesus Christ is Savior who transforms us into his own glorious body by virtue of that dynamism that enables him to subject everything to himself." Here Paul sums up his inner experience with himself, with the world, and with Christ. Paul has experienced that there is nothing in himself or in the world that the love of Christ cannot subject and transform into itself. Paul has come to know that there is not one secret that he has or is aware of or is unaware of in himself or in the world that the love of Christ cannot subject unto itself. Paul has become aware that there is no weakness within him or problem or difficulty or darkness or evil or conflict within him or in the world that is deeper or more powerful than the love of Christ.

> Nothing therefore can come between us and the love of Christ, even if we are troubled or worried, or being perse-cuted, or lacking food or clothes, or being threatened or even attacked. These are the trials through which we tri-umph, by the power of him who loved us.
>
> For I am certain of this: neither death nor life, no angel, no prince, nothing that exists, nothing still to come, not any power, or height or depth, nor any created thing, can ever come between us and the love of God made visible in Christ Jesus our Lord. (Rom 8:35–39)

Discussion Questions

What is spirituality?

What is the divine arena of action?

What is the meaning of weakness in the experience of St. Paul? Have you experienced this?

How is God present in your experience of weakness?

Do you experience God in the experience of your own weakness?

What is God saying to you in your life now?

What is your spirituality that is emerging from your life experience of God?

What does the spiritual life mean to you?

How does Paul's experience of weakness to strength enlighten and inform the experience of changing bad habits to good habits in Christ?

CHAPTER NINE

Weakness and Spirituality

The object of this volume is not to answer all of your questions about spirituality but to present a dialogue partner for you. I am attempting to present a phenomenal field for you to experience and find yourself. I am presenting a horizon on which you can place yourself and your own experience and so understand your own inner experience...your own inner journey. I hope this consideration is a travel partner for you as you respond to God in your life.

To come to grips better with a notion of spirituality, it helps to investigate another example of a human being dealing with God: St. John of the Cross, a sixteenth-century Carmelite priest. This study will be supported and supplemented by the experience of St. Ignatius of Loyola.

The experience Paul refers to in his own life as "weakness" St. John of the Cross refers to as his "dark night of the soul." The temperament, environment, and social milieu of these two individuals differ radically. The apostolic expression and response of these two disciples of Christ vary accordingly. There is a constant, however: the identifiable hand of God. The instrumentality is very different. The personality of the individuals, the social conditions they find themselves in, the expressional modes of action born of each history, upbringing, and education are very different.[149]

To help clarify this, we will use the "First Principle and Foundation" of the *Spiritual Exercises* of St. Ignatius Loyola, the founder of the Society of Jesus, the Jesuits. This order of the church had its origin in his conversion experience at his Basque ancestral home in 1521. Ignatius had been a worldly man in every way until faced with convalescence from a battle injury. God entered his life while Ignatius read the Scriptures, lives of the saints, and the *Life of Christ* by Ludolf of Saxony. Ignatius surrendered his life to the call of Christ. He spent a year at Manresa in Spain struggling with the movements of deep despair over his past life and the euphoric consolations of God's graces.

Ignatius found that writing down his experiences of despair and hopelessness over his past life, the thoughts that came from these, and the resultant feelings gave him relief. He then did the same with the love and deep devotion he received from the hand of God, the thoughts that proceeded from those consolations, and the resultant feelings as well. As he wrote and wrote, he realized an ever deeper relief and clarity. His writings during that year have come down to us as his *Spiritual Exercises*.

God's hand, for Paul and for John, can be broadly expressed as God's movement into their lives as God, the Creator of the world, the Lord of the universe, and their own personal savior and lover. For these individuals, God's hand in their lives corresponded to Ignatius's "First Principle and Foundation."

> Every person is created to praise and reverence, and serve God our Lord, and by this means to save their soul.
>
> The other things on the face of the earth were created for their sake, and in order to aid them in the attaining of the end to which they were created.
>
> So it follows that every person must make use of them insofar as they help them to attain their end, and in the same way they ought to withdraw themselves from them insofar as they hinder them from it.
>
> It is therefore necessary that we should make ourselves indifferent to all created things, insofar as it is left to the liberty of our free will to do so, and is not forbidden; in such sort that we do not for our part wish for health rather than sickness, for wealth rather than poverty, for honour rather than dishonour, for a long life rather than a short one; and so in all other things.
>
> Our one desire and choice should be what will most lead us to the end for which we were created.[150]

God came to Paul and John as God, their Creator; they considered themselves created by God and servants to their Creator. How did this knowledge and union come to each? It can be seen from what has preceded that St. Paul was brought to knowledge and union through the instrumentality of being "sent to prison," "whipped almost to death," "beaten with sticks," "stoned," "shipwrecked," subjected to "hunger and thirst and often starving," and other sufferings. Paul knew that God was coming to him in a way that was so true and real, even though he did not understand it, that he "gloried in his weakness." Paul rejoiced and looked upon his struggles as a joy because God would glorify him in his weakness. Paul rejoiced in his weakness and inability, as it allowed God's grace to work easily through and in him.

St. John of the Cross in his poem *The Dark Night* refers to how he came to this knowledge and union with God:

> One dark night,
> Fired with love's urgent longing
> —Ah, the sheer grace!—
> I went out unseen,
> My house being now all stilled;
>
> In darkness, and secure,
> By the secret ladder, disguised,
> —Ah, the sheer grace!—
> In darkness and concealment,
> My house being now all stilled;
>
> On that glad night
> In secret, for no one saw me,
> Nor did I look at anything,
> With no other light or guide
> Than the one that burned in my heart;
>
> This guided me
> More surely than the light of noon
> To where He waited for me
> —Him I knew so well—
> In a place where no one else appeared.
>
> Oh guiding night!
> O night more lovely than the dawn!

O night that has united
The lover with his beloved,
Transforming the beloved in her lover.[151]

"The hand of God comes to John of the Cross through the instrumentality of his contemplative prayer life."[152] John experiences as difficult his own choice of being with Christ in poverty, chastity, and obedience. The pain of consciously choosing the motivation of the glory of God instead of the immediate gratification of one's senses upon perceiving their desired object is obvious in his treatment of the beginning stages of "purgation." This he does by composing and analyzing the poem he wrote, *The Dark Night,* from the point of view of the active choice of the individual to choose actual poverty, chastity, and obedience. This consideration is entitled *The Ascent of Mount Carmel.* Here John speaks of a person's deep desire to do only God's will. Feeling called to the evangelical counsels, a person leaves the world—the immediate gratification of one's sense desires and impulses. This is a sort of "dark night." "This denial and privation is like a night for all one's senses."[153] The reason for this is that the senses must defer their gratification to another source or cause—the glory of God—as perceived by the intellect, as John presents it. When a person chooses to enter this journey, the means of travel is faith. Faith is a dark-night experience for a person's rationality.[154] Why? Because the active night of the senses means the rupture of the immediate relationship of sense perception to its object and gratification—ideas, concepts, images—by the motive of *faith*. What does faith give a person that causes blindness for these perceptions? An unknown object! Faith gives us an unproportional object: God. Things a person knows are radically reapportioned. The horizon of a person's phenomenal field of perception now is God. Before faith a person perceives things with God: apples, oranges, God, and peanuts. Now in faith a person perceives all things in God: apples, oranges, and peanuts *coming from God*. All is now perceived on the horizon of God. Here the ontology of the universe is not falsified, but the truth is perceived. Faith here blinds us by illuminating much the same way as the sun blinds the eyes of a sick person as a nurse opens the curtains to the morning. John of the Cross is not talking here of emptying oneself of all sense and intellectual perceptions, objects, or concepts. This is not a privation of object or faculty but of the immediate gratification of one's ability and perception with its object. It is a detachment or freedom from spontaneous gratification in sense objects, concepts, and ideas as a guide or support along the road to union with the will of God. The only guide or support John seeks is faith. The point of arrival is the very self of God. The way to this experience of God is a dark night for humanity in this life, for God communicates God's very self secretly and intimately to women and men.[155]

A person walks to God in faith alone at this point. This means walking in "darkness" for the habits, powers, and abilities of a person and in an illumination of the powers beyond one's natural capabilities. Here are uncovered in a person seeking to walk this road to union with God an undeviating thirst, hunger, and direction toward God rather than the experience of God: a choosing of God, not of the words of God or the visions of God. This is the desire to abandon oneself to God alone. Here is a movement toward choosing God for God's own sake, a choosing of God with no feedback, a choosing of God and not of what God can feed back to me in my life.[156]

At this point God moves to purify the intent of the traveler. This process is the content of *The Dark Night*. John's poem describes an experience with two aspects: an active one and a passive one. The active aspect is the one just described, where I act by choosing the motive. The passive aspect entails what is done by God to me and in me. God enters the soul to purify its resolve by aridity and sterility, by a sense of dryness and a feeling of being separated from its Lord and God.

How does one know when one is undergoing this passive dark night of the senses and spirit? How does one know when one is undergoing a condition directly caused by the hand of God? This can best be seen in light of the signs for recognizing the active dark night of the senses.[157] The instrumentality of communication for John of the Cross between himself and God was contemplative prayer. When in contemplative prayer one cannot make discursive meditation (prayer using words, imagination, concepts, ideas, fantasy), when one does not receive any satisfaction from such prayer, one can suspect that one must change the focus of one's senses in prayer to a new source. Dryness is now the outcome of the habit of fixing one's senses upon the subjects that formerly provided satisfaction.[158] Another sign is a rising awareness of an aversion and disinclination to fix one's imagination or senses upon other particular objects. The truest and surest sign is that a person likes to remain alone in loving awareness of God, without particular considerations, in interior peace and quiet and repose, and without the acting and exercises of the senses, intellect, memory, and will.[159] These three signs must be observed together for this change to be authentic. It is possible that the inability to meditate may be caused by one's "dissipation and lack of diligence."[160] When this is caused by laziness, one tends to distractions and likes distracting thoughts and fantasies. This is not the case in one who is earnestly seeking union with God. The sign of loving knowledge and peaceful awareness is necessary to render the experience genuine because "the cause could be melancholia or some other kind of humor in the heart or brain capable of producing a certain stupefaction and suspension of the sense faculties."[161] These three signs apply to the active night of the senses.

The signs for perceiving the passive dark night of the senses can be reduced to aridity. Here God is entering one's prayer life to purify one's motive of love of God. This aridity has its own characteristics. The first sign that one traveling this road experiences is no consolation or satisfaction from prayer life. God is here putting a person's soul in this dark night to dry up and purge his or her sensory appetite, as John would say. This can be determined to be the action of God if there is no propensity to find satisfaction in sensory objects felt in the sensory part of the soul.[162] The second sign is necessary if this is to be the authentic action of God, for this aridity may be caused by some disposition that prevents one from being satisfied with anything. The second sign is that if one starts to remember the things of God, how God has dealt with one's soul, and carefully seeks out God thinking and feeling that such aridity must be the soul's fault and thinking its aversion for God means it has turned back on this road, it is obvious that the aridity is not from laziness. A "lax, tepid, or lazy person" does not care for the attention of God. A "lax or tepid person" is usually lazy in will and spirit and is not intent on serving God. A person going through this dark night is very concerned about serving God and pained at not doing so. Psychological indispositions very often accompany and color this aridity. If the aridity is caused solely by psychological causes, the aridity ends in disgust, and none of the desires to serve God accompany the aridity.[163] In the aridity of the dark night, while the sensory part of the soul is weakened, the spirit is nourished, becoming ready and strong. The spirit grows in its intent on serving and never failing God. The third sign, then, is that one's spirit feels the strength and energy to work. The conduct of a person in this dark night of the senses is to remain quiet and without care about any interior or exterior work with one's senses or emotions or rational abilities.[164] This activity would hinder rather than help God's activity of binding the rational and emotional powers by instilling God's own delicate, solitary, and satisfying peace and loving knowledge of God's very self. The fourth sign of this passive dark night of the senses initiated by God is one's inability "to meditate and make use of the imagination" as one was able to do before.[165] God communicates God's very self "through pure spirit by an act of simple contemplation, in which there is no discursive succession of thought."[166] From this sign one can see that the aridity does not come from psychological causes, for, if it did, one would be able to return at will to the beneficial meditating one had been accustomed to.[167] In this dark night initiated by God, the powerlessness to meditate continues. One traveling toward union with God is now in the hands of God. One's own ability to effect change is nonexistent. What one used to do does not work anymore. The person is being drawn by God into a union with the will of God that can be achieved only by the activity of God alone.[168]

This process-experience is called a dark night by John of the Cross because the knowledge of God is such wisdom that it exceeds the capacity of the soul, just as the sun blinds and darkens our eyes as we look at it.[169] This light of God causes pain in the soul upon reception, as does the sun upon sick eyes. Such persons feel as though they are unclean and unloved by God. They feel that God is against them and that they are against God. In the pure light of God's loving knowledge, they see their own insufficiencies and inadequacies. They feel helplessly immersed in their own difficulties. These miseries are brought into relief "so that the soul sees clearly that of itself it will never possess anything else."[170]

John of the Cross describes some of the dangers at this point along the spiritual path. He speaks of the spiritual apprehension and feelings received. He calls this state that of proficients, not beginners, and maintains that this lasts for a long period of time, often years. The Lord here accustoms the traveler to spiritual comprehensions. The sensory part of the soul weakens as the proficient develops and works and labors for the glory of God. Here the proficient can become wedded to his or her spiritual delights and perceptions, becoming too secure in surrender and abandonment to them. The Lord now introduces the soul to aridity and the absence of such spiritual communications so that the soul is made to walk in the darkness of pure faith, "the proper and adequate means to divine union."[171]

Discussion Questions

"Darkness" for St. John of the Cross is the pain we feel when our accustomed stimulus-response, need-gratification pattern physically or emotionally is interrupted or stopped because of a decision we make to follow Christ. This is a "dark night" for our usual habits and experiences. Have you ever experienced this?

The active dark night for St. John of the Cross is the experience of choosing how I will follow Christ. Have you ever been in charge of your spiritual life? What has that been like for you?

The passive dark night for St. John of the Cross is the experience of God taking charge of you and your spiritual life by God's action. Have you ever experienced that?

What has that been like for you?

How has that come about in your life?

CHAPTER TEN

The Passion of Divine Love

In this night the sensory part of the soul and the spirit are jointly purified. In its movement toward union with God, what yet needs to be purified in the sensory part of the soul has its roots in the spirit. During the dark night the spirit is purged so that the sensory part is purified at its roots.

> God divests the faculties, affections, and senses, both spiritual and sensory, interior and exterior. He leaves the intellect in darkness, the will in aridity, the memory in emptiness, and the affections in supreme affliction, bitterness, and anguish by depriving the soul of the feeling and satisfaction it previously obtained from spiritual blessings.[172]

The reason God does this is to introduce the spiritual form of love, the union of love, into the spirit of a person and unite with it. The means that God uses to do this is dark contemplation. God uses the instrumentality of the contemplative's prayer life. What this means for the rational and sensual powers and faculties is torment and darkness.[173] The soul is impressed with an intimate sense of its own poverty, weakness, and misery. The soul experiences emptiness and is conscious of its imperfections, aridities, and voids in the apprehensions of the faculties, and of an abandonment of the spirit in darkness. The intellect devoid of conceptual objects is in darkness as it walks in faith. The will suffers great sorrow in that it knows how far from the service of God it really is.[174] Persons in this state find no comfort or support from any doctrine or spiritual director. At this point, if a spiritual director explains this condition to the souls, they believe the director does not understand them. They believe the spiritual director does not see or feel what they feel.[175] Their sorrow deepens, as they believe no one can help them or understand them. Their memory now is darkened, as they believe that their affliction will not end. They are devoid of hope. They remain in this state until their spirit "becomes so delicate, simple and refined that it can be one with the Spirit of God."[176]

God does this to persons seeking union with God "only that one may reach out divinely to the enjoyment of all earthly and heavenly things, with a general freedom of spirit in them all."[177] John here discusses the enkindling of love in the spirit of a person. Now the soul has a certain feeling and foretaste of God, understanding nothing, however.

The spirit now experiences "an impassioned and intense love"[178]—a passion of love. This love is infused and engenders a strong passion of love for God in the soul. The soul is equipped to receive this love, as all of its sensory and rational powers are unable to be satisfied by any heavenly or earthly thing. God has prepared all the soul's strength and all its sensory and rational powers, as it is not scattered by its satisfaction in other things. It is now ready to be taken up in love of its Creator and Lord. The goal of this whole process is to gather "together all the strength, faculties, and appetites of the soul, spiritual and sensory alike, that the energy and the power of this whole harmonious composite may be employed in this love."[179] This state is a fulfillment of the first commandment, "You shall love the Lord, your God, with all your heart, with all your soul, and with all your strength" (Mark 12:30).

John continues his development in the poem *The Living Flame of Love*. His commentary on this poem is in the form of a book bearing the same name. John uses the metaphor of a flame for the Holy Spirit's presence. The flame is an assimilative principle making everything it comes in contact with like itself. He likens the soul of a person to a log. The Spirit of God, the living flame, touches the soul, the log, to transform the log into itself. As a flame first dries out a log in a fire, so the Spirit does to the soul until the log itself is sending up flames of its own.[180] Now the soul itself burns with the love of God radiating and flaming its own fire of love. The union with divine love has taken place. The living flame of love now burns; the soul now burns with the same love. Union has been effected. John here communicates this experience:

> O living flame of love
> That tenderly wounds my soul
> In its deepest center. Since
> Now You are not oppressive,
> Now Consummate! if it be Your will:
> Tear through the veil of this sweet encounter!
>
> O sweet cautery,
> O delightful wound!
> O gentle hand! O delicate touch
> That tastes of eternal life
> And pays every debt!
> In killing You changed death to life.
>
> O lamps of fire!
> In whose splendors
> The deep caverns of feeling…
> Once obscure and blind
> Now give forth, so rarely, so exquisitely,
> Both warmth and light to their Beloved.
>
> How gently and lovingly
> You woke in my heart
> Where in secret You dwell alone;
> And in Your sweet breathing,
> Filled with good and glory,
> How tenderly You swell my heart with love.[181]

John comments on the last stanza of his poem in the most brief manner: "I do not desire to speak of this spiration, filled for the soul with good and glory and delicate love of God, for I am aware of being incapable of so doing, and were I to try, it might seem less than it is. The Holy Spirit, through this breathing, filled the soul with good and glory, in which He enkindled it in love of Himself, indescribably and incomprehensibly, in the depths of God, to Whom be honor and glory forever and ever. Amen."[182] John simply leaves here his description of the joys and depths of the love God infuses into a soul as beyond words and description.

In *The Dark Night* John explains what a secure and reliable means of travel the soul has in darkness. A soul never strays or loses its way except through its compulsive sensorial life or through its own discursive meditation relying on its own images and concepts, knowledge and affections. These powers impeded, one finds oneself liberated from them and also from error through them.[183] The sensory and rational capabilities in a person are good. God created them. The natural objects of these powers are also good. God created them. God enters in and impedes the operation of these powers to infuse God's own divine love and wisdom as the operating and motivating experience and principle of action. This process necessitates the reception of spiritual love by the spirit of persons on this journey. In this they are strengthened as they exercise themselves by walking courageously forward in the darkness of all their senses and rational powers. As the spirit exercises itself and accustoms itself to itself, it grows in its capability to receive infused divine love.[184] The senses and rational powers, completely darkened and without any of their object gratification, unencumbered and free, can now join in and receive divine love. Now the sensory and rational capabilities not only can become participatory with respect to receiving divine love but can become expressional mediums as well.

Here we can return to a previous quote from John of the Cross for additional insight. God does this "only that one may reach out divinely to the enjoyment of all earthly and heavenly things, with a general freedom of spirit in them all."[185] God darkens one's capabilities and infuses God's divine love and vision into one only to give back all of one's sensory, rational, and human abilities.[186] God gives them back, however, with an added dimension: a "general freedom of spirit in them all." This general freedom is a direct result of the infusion of divine love. Now the soul is so sure of its deepest center and fulfillment, union with the will of God, that it seeks nothing else first. All other things on the face of the earth are simply all other things on the horizon of God. They are not God. They are to be treated as what they are: created, creatures, as the "First Principle and Foundation" of St. Ignatius's *Spiritual Exercises* expresses it. So a general freedom has arisen in the person in union with his or her Creator and Lord. The freedom is in respect to everything on the face of the earth. This is the "freedom of the Children of God" (Rom 8:21).

This process for St. John of the Cross has entered deep into his psychological emotional life. John has encountered God and dealt with God through the medium of his own contemplative prayer life, and he now has a general freedom toward all things. He now experiences a general freedom to move in any direction upon any eventuality. John has become from this experience a person of deep love and compassion rooted in the presence of the love of his Beloved.

Discussion Questions

Have you ever experienced a sense of being far from God even though you wanted to serve God? What was this like?

Have you experienced being unable to derive consolation or comfort from any explanation of a spiritual director? Share with your group.

Have you experienced a sense that your affliction will never end? How does that feel?

What does it mean that God does this in order to give us back everything with a general freedom toward it all?

When our powers are impeded, God infuses divine love. Have you experienced this? Discuss in your group.

PART FOUR

Divine Union

CHAPTER ELEVEN

Spirituality and Personality

I believe we are ready at this point to see some similarities and dissimilarities between St. Paul's movement toward God and that of St. John of the Cross. Some similarities can also be seen between these saints' expressions of this development in their experience.

St. Paul was called to be the "apostle of the gentiles." He lived his life after his conversion preaching the word of the Lord Jesus to women and men in the world who had never heard such discourse. This was the way that Paul felt he had to work out his inner call and feelings. This was Paul's expression of his love of Christ, the desire of his life. In speaking this word, Paul met opposition from within himself, from other men and women, and from the "spirit of evil." Paul expresses this experience as a battle. He is constantly besieged by his own inner inability to do what he wants to do. Paul finds he does exactly what he does not want to do. "I cannot understand my own behavior. I fail to carry out the things I want to do. And I find myself doing the very things I do not want to do" (Rom 7:15–16). He is faced with inner confusion and disorganization. Paul barges through this "in the faith of Jesus Christ." Paul here experiences the capability to forgive himself and accept his weaknesses. He finds himself rejoicing as he rests in faith. Paul forgives himself upon the strength of God's grace yet does not use this forgiveness as an excuse for not doing what he can to remedy his own incapabilities. Paul then faces the army of women and men who believe he is imbalanced, dangerous, and evil for saying and doing what he does. Paul faces women and men who exert direct physical, emotional, and intellectual force and pressure against him. He is beaten, imprisoned, ostracized, and argued against. Paul, beaten and weary, becomes strengthened and powerful in trust and hope in the power of Christ to work through and effect love. This happens—his own darkness notwithstanding. Paul here experiences a darkness to all his senses and rational powers. All of Paul's human notions of "how to do it" and of how to communicate the word of the Lord are darkened either by his own weakness or by the plain and simple opposition of those to whom he speaks. This darkness is illuminated only by the faith, hope, and love that Jesus Christ infuses into the soul and person of Paul. Because of Paul's situation, he is very aware of the source of the darkness: Christ Jesus. Paul rejoices in this and can say he looks upon his own weakness as his dearest experience, for it is the occasion of the coming of the Lord (2 Cor 12:9).

Paul's "weakness" seems here to have the same meaning to him as "darkness" has to St. John of the Cross. Weakness for Paul is the condition of total impotence and inability of his own human powers to effect any qualitative change or grace of God within his given situation. Paul rejoices in his weakness.

John of the Cross calls his darkness a "glad night": "O guiding night! O night more lovely than the dawn, O night that has united the Lover with His beloved."[187] St. John of the Cross rejoices in his darkness, for in it the Lord came and comes. For both Paul and John, this impedance of their sensory and rational powers was overcome by a growing and strengthened power of faith, hope, and love of Christ Jesus. This experience for both of them was infused by God. In their lives they each returned to all things with a general freedom toward everything. In their lives they each began by choosing the will of God instead of the immediate gratification of their own emotional sensory and rational powers. Gradually their own lives were taken out of their own hands, so that they each found the hand of God purifying them rather than their own active purifying of themselves. The hand of God purified them to a degree they could not have done by themselves. They each found themselves infused with the divine love for God, themselves, and the world.

For both Paul and John, the experience of meeting God and their ensuing experiences with God affected their entire lives. They are changed persons. They both have been freed by the love of God to love themselves, others, and all creation with all of their human capabilities. They are free and loving persons. God's presence and action in their lives have brought their personalities "to full stature." This hand of God, for both Paul and John, is not so strange when viewed in terms of human interaction. There comes a time when a mother says to her little child, "It's time to walk now." She has been carrying her child from room to room, from house to car, from store to store. Then, one day, it dawns on her like instinct, "Today it's time for you to walk." The little child first frowns and gets angry and then starts to cry. The child says in its feelings, "If you really loved me, you'd pick me up and carry me." The little child feels rejected and angry, and in its little body it feels nothing but pain as it begins to struggle to walk. The little child feels pain and anger. It feels weakness and frustration. The little child notes that its mother is causing it this pain by demanding that it walk. The little child says again, "If you loved me, you wouldn't ask me to do this; you'd carry me." The truth is, however, that the little child's judgment and conclusion are inaccurate. The little child's mother does love it. The little child's mother simply wants it to walk, to grow, to run, to ride a bike, to dance, and to walk away eventually from her to its own life. The mother wants her child to be free. She knows, however, that her little child must walk in order to do this growing. So she asks this of her child. Pain, anger, and frustration are the result in her child. The child must "walk" through this "darkness" within its familiar pattern of feelings, body movements, and bodily living. This is a dark and painful road for the little child. The mother shows her love for her child by introducing this new reality of walking to the child and by not picking up the child even though it causes darkness and suffering for her child. This is exactly what God is doing here. God is bringing Paul and John to full stature, full freedom, and full love as they walk in weakness and darkness toward God, growing as they walk.

There was darkness in Paul and John's emotional lives as they walked on in faith alone. God gave them each back their emotional lives and their entire lives now with a freedom and love built on God's infused love.

There is much evidence for a dissimilarity between the movement of Paul toward God and that of John of the Cross. The difference is the means through which and by which the Lord actively purified each of these individuals, preparing them for the infusion of God's own love. The means chosen by God to come to these two persons is their own individual personalities: their emotional, intellectual, and personal makeups, capabilities, desires, and personhoods. Paul was called by Christ to be an active apostolic missionary to the Jews and the gentiles. This was his vocation. The instrumentality used by God to come to Paul was Paul's own extroverted, expressive, and aggressive emotionality surging out into the world to confront and engage women and men directly. Paul was a person of the world who knew his way around it and was comfortable and naturally challenged by it. The Lord called Paul to the world in this direct way and used everything in the world to obstruct Paul's own reliance upon it and upon himself in a spontaneously naïve way. The Lord gave back Paul's powers and all created things in the world with a general freedom toward them all, and Paul was buoyed by the divine love God infused into him.

John of the Cross was called by Christ to a contemplative vocation of prayer. The instrumentality used by God to come to John of the Cross was John's contemplative prayer life, his own deep running emotionality, his temperateness of activity, his intellectual acumen, his love of poetry, and his own deep interest and fascination with the inner life of human beings.[188] John found the completion and full expression of his own being in a life of prayer and solitude as a Carmelite. God used the instrumentality of contemplative prayer to meet and infuse God's own divine love into John. In John's prayer the Lord actively accomplished this by impeding John's sensory and rational powers.

Both John and Paul can say with St. Ignatius of Loyola that they were made for God and that all things were created by God. With Ignatius they can say that the things on the face of the earth are to be used for this purpose, now their own purpose, the love of God.[189] Both of these individuals were saints traveling the long, difficult, and joyous road to union with God. They traveled to the same God in the same direction, but their roads each wound through their own selfhood and personality. The hand of God can be seen in that the Creator's own respect for God's creation is present: two human beings with very different personalities, lifestyles, histories, and environments. These two human beings were touched by their Creator in the same way through different avenues, with each personality left peacefully intact.

Discussion Questions

What are the similarities and dissimilarities between the lives and experiences of St. Paul and St. John of the Cross?

What are the similarities and dissimilarities between their lives and your own life?

Have you experienced not doing what you want to do but doing what you do not want to do? Even after years of prayer? What does this experience mean to you in your spiritual life?

The previous questions concern inner opposition to God's love and call. Have you experienced outer opposition? What was that experience like for you? Share in your group.

Were you weak in this experience of outer opposition? How so?

Is this weakness the same as darkness? Was this experience your dark night?

CHAPTER TWELVE

The Purification of Interior Habits

Part 2 of this book described an experience human to the core, its development, and its therapeutic resolution. Part 3 looked at two human experiences: Paul, a contemplative in action, and John, a contemplative. We began part 4 by looking at how these two experiences were really one in their essence, direction, and movement. We saw how different human personalities were met by God on their own different terms through their own different life experiences.

We now raise this question: Is emotional suffering spiritual? Is the emotional pain and suffering endured by persons as they move from deep unconscious pain to psychological health through the process of psychotherapy the spiritual life? The same question can be phrased thus: Is the psychotherapeutic struggle the spiritual life? How can our Christian traveler seeking God look on his or her struggles with unconscious emotional feelings as that spiritual search? Do the experiences of St. Paul and St. John of the Cross have anything to say to our contemporary Christian pilgrim seeking God? I think they do.

The experience of emotional suffering and resolution as the spiritual life can be seen from the elements of the emotional therapeutic dynamics I have described and from the basic dynamic elements in the spiritualities of St. Paul and St. John of the Cross. This process begins with a synthetic exposé of emotional suffering.

When our pilgrim experiencing emotional suffering comes to the counselor-guide for assistance, the former is sincerely in the dark with respect to what is bothering him or her. Our pilgrim's notions are vague and general. The process of psychotherapy is very dark and painful. It is a journey into the unknown. It is a search for what one has really never known: oneself. This journey is into one's own unconscious to free oneself from all hidden and unmanageable emotions and unresolved conflicts.[190] Commencing this process, our pilgrim waits at this abyss of the very self with usually one insightful feeling: fear.

> One is faced with their conflicts and the hideous fear of being torn to pieces. That this may give one a chance of becoming a much better human being, worth more than all the glory of one's idealized image, is a gospel they hear but that for a long time means nothing to them. It is a leap in the dark of which they are afraid.[191]

This fear reaches back to the original fear the traveler had and still has with regard to allowing the self to feel the feelings he or she originally had felt. Psychotherapy uncovers the feelings the traveler is feeling at present. This process is a very dark, scary, painful, and fearful experience for a person, as the whole conscious dynamic has been to block the free flow of any feeling, be it love, or joy, or need, or fear, or sorrow, or anger. The interior of a feeling issuing from the real self to the world of real people cuts deeply the emotional membranes of a carefully constructed defense. This is utter pain, torment, affliction, and suffering to the kept-in-check interior of the individual. The traveler's familiar interior emotional modes of feeling are giving way to unfamiliar, new, and unknown impulses that seem to touch an explosive-like morass of feeling within. "Can I allow this?" the person wonders. "What if I do? Won't I explode if I come in contact with what I'm really feeling? I'll lose control of myself." All of these questions point up the suffering and uncertainty of the person walking the road toward emotional health.

Following the typical experience as presented earlier, the vagueness and "something's wrong" feeling of the person will show itself as suffering in terms of guilt, shame, or inferiority. This has been the safest way to handle feelings—or so the traveler has thought. A basic incongruence between the vocal script read and the sensed body language usually will show itself, giving the concerned helper a handle by which to pry open and begin to dislodge the traveler's set of lifelong, carefully built defense-mechanistic habitual statements about himself or herself.[192] As a counselor-guide begins, through his or her own techniques, to point out these incongruencies of script and behavior, the confusion caused in the person's mind and emotions is very high and painful. This confusion is compounded by fear. Upon the reality contact with a counselor, the self-concept rushes to represent the self through the individual's habitual script. The real self rushes to reality through the body. The two collide. This is a painful conflict. This is a personal emotional conflict.[193] At this point confusion reigns, as the counselor-guide has pointed up a symptom of the person's personality disorganization. This confusion is darkness and suffering for our traveler. What do the darkness and suffering affect in the individual? The darkness and suffering affect the entire habit of his or her defense-mechanistic system, as the traveler has been hard at work to have it function fully as protection against feeling any real-self emotion. It is darkness therefore for the person's living self-concept, darkness for all of the reality, value, and possibility assumptions the individual has of his or her self. This is a very real darkness and suffering for our traveler. The person in our example-story has been living for so long emotionally running away from feeling real-self hate for his or her life frustration, his or her parents, that the individual has become unconscious of the real self and real-self feelings. Our pilgrim, in turn, has become conscious of the self he or she has constructed—a complexus of reality, value, and possibility assumptions that are not rooted in the real self but are rooted in what the person thinks they should be. This is a self rooted in what others think one should be, not in one's real selfhood. At this point the traveler's rational capabilities believe the constructed self, the self-concept, to actually be the real self. The challenge of the counselor-guide causes confusion and darkness to the traveler's self-concept because the counselor-guide has pointed out nonverbal body behavior that says something different from the verbal content expressed.[194] This fact when attempted to be adverted to by the individual—whether any understanding is forthcoming to the traveler or not at that time— begins to cast darkness upon the self-constructed reality, value, and possibility assumptions held so dearly and tightly by our traveler. "Maybe I'm not this way...maybe I can't do this...maybe I don't really want this...maybe what I thought I should do isn't for me."

These maybes, these doubts, mean darkness and suffering for the intellectual beliefs our traveler has used as the foundation for reality contact. For reality contact, the self-concept has acted as a defense. This construct has not simply been conceptual or intellectual in nature. As emotions are spontaneous and automatic feeling responses to reality, there exist here in the self-concept many automatic emotional responses to the contained reality, value, and possibility assumptions conceptually conceived.[195] These emotional habits and responses have become ingrained. They have spontaneously responded to the hopes, dreams, and values presented to them by the self-concept for such a long period of time that they have worn an emotional path and groove deep into the traveler's very being. They are bad habits. The counselor-guide points up body behavior that is symptomatic of other emotions that have been repressed yet still exist. This challenge spells darkness for the long-felt, familiar, and safe emotions. The reason this is darkness and suffering for the conscious emotions is that the traveler is leaving them. The traveler is beginning to leave the familiar habits and patterns of emoting and feeling. The reason for this is the darkness at the conceptual level of perception to which the traveler's emotions have spontaneously responded. This is darkness for the traveler's intellect because one is leaving one's self-concept. The traveler is beginning to leave what he or she thought the self to be. This is a dark and powerful journey...dark and powerful for the traveler's mind...dark and powerful for the emotions. This is not only a dark journey in night because of what one is leaving; there is a darkness as to what one is moving toward. One does not know through what means to find oneself. One does not know what one will find when the journey has ended and one has found oneself. This is why the whole process of psychotherapy is dark and a "night" for the traveler.

The counselor-guide, observing incongruencies between the verbal and nonverbal behavior of the traveler, mentions his or her observations to the traveler, attempting to bring this into the latter's awareness. As this experience proceeds, the traveler is led to asking questions as to the origin, source, and cause of his or her disordered affection, their bad habit. Our pilgrim asks, "How did this come about? How did this come to be?" This part of our traveler's journey is very dark and painful. It is an embarkation into one's unconscious. It is an attempt to uncover the experiences that caused such a flood of emotion within the now suffering person that the person could not stabilize the self normally. He or she had to flee through the means of repression.[196]

As this proceeds, the cognitive labeling and its psychodynamic underpinnings, all pointing to the suffering as feelings of guilt, shame, and inferiority, begin to evanesce. This takes place as one loses confidence in one's self-concept as being the true representation of one's selfhood. As this takes place, the self-concept defense-mechanistic habit cannot label the as yet undifferentiated feelings of anxiety as guilt, shame, and inferiority as well as it used to. The reason for this is the as yet unrecognizable emergence of the real self as the healthy self…the vibrant self…the "savior on the horizon." The traveler, making his or her way in darkness, in affliction and torment, feels nothing but pain and suffering with reference to all former perception. The traveler experiences this as the spiritual within. The eighteenth-century Jesuit Jean-Pierre de Caussade in *Abandonment to Divine Providence* uses the image of a stone experiencing a sculptor's blows:

> Each blow from the harmony of the sculptor's chisel makes it feel—if it could—as if it was being destroyed. As blow after blow descends, the stone knows nothing of how the sculptor is shaping it. All it feels is a chisel chopping away at it cutting and mutilating it.[197]

Yet the traveler's movement to seek freedom and health and his or her persistence in the face of onslaughts on the self-concept by the counselor-guide have fortified the traveler and called deeply to the real self to "come out and play." The real self hears this call and begins to answer, no matter how buried it is. The dammed-up condition of the sufferer is breaking loose. The traveler is now capable of receiving and of responding emotionally in a spontaneous way that was unattainable in his or her development to this point. This means encouragement and emotional strength to our pilgrim. This "light in the darkness" acts as motivation to continue the journey into one's feelings, one's unconscious, and one's past. The fear in this venture is all-embracive. The darkness and suffering deepen the nearer the traveler gets to the explosive-like morass of feelings he or she senses to be at the finality of this journey. The traveler approaches this dark pit upon the rising awareness, within the very self, of being indeed lovable and loving. This awareness becomes more prominent the more the log-jammed self-concept is picked apart by the counselor-guide, releasing spontaneously the real self. This rising dynamic awareness brings the traveler to the edge of the pit of unknown feeling. The traveler embraces anger. The traveler peers fearfully yet unhesitatingly into his or her own feelings of anger. "It is all right to feel anger," the traveler concludes. "It is all right for me to feel anger. It is all right for my self to be in my body, in my consciousness, in my awareness as angry." At this juncture the traveler has faced the conflict that is the source of his or her false-self defense-mechanistic habit.[198] The traveler has looked into the darkness and again been consoled. "What to do with this anger?" emerges as the next question. The answer is to express the feeling to whomever the feeling is aimed. The traveler is now faced with confronting the significant others of youth, his or her parents, with this feeling. It means the proper expression of a feeling the traveler has considered for years to be improper. This is a dark and painful journey; yet strengthened by previous successes, the traveler proceeds into the darkness with some hope and confidence. As this process of feeling vaguely that something is wrong, asking oneself what one is feeling and why, discovering the answer, and, finally, expressing it to whom the feeling is aimed becomes habitual, the traveler comes to walk the road of life alone. Our traveler's need to rely on psychotherapy and a counselor-guide evanesces. Our pilgrim is free.

Discussion Questions

Have you experienced the movement from being outer directed to being inner directed? What is this like for you?

Is self-concept living disordered affection? Why?

Is living from a false self-concept a bad habit? How?

Is the fear of giving up self-concept living and moving to real-self living a dark night for a person?

Is changing ingrained emotional behavior penance, mortification, and abnegation?

Is changing interior bad habits to good habits inner pennance?

CHAPTER THIRTEEN

Glad Night:
The Emergence of Freedom

This journey in retrospect is looked at by the traveler as "a glad night,…a night more lovely than the dawn."[199] Upon arrival at the emotional stage of the emergence of the real self, the traveler sees the necessity of walking the painful and dark road of moving from outer-directed false-self conceptual reactions to inner-directed real-self reactions. This journey was made in darkness, and as John of the Cross says, the result has made the darkness sweet. This journey was made in darkness, pain, and suffering to our pilgrim's self-concept: his or her reality, value, and possibility assumptions. It was from this false self-concept that the pilgrim related to the world. This way of living was destroyed by the counselor-guide's observations. The false self-concept thus became impotent as a means of effecting any creative change for the person. The traveler's self-concept was being darkened, rendered incapable of producing any real-self actualizing qualities of joy or reward or any real emotional "stick to the ribs" experience. With the traveler's frame of perception incapable of effecting the resolution of any emotional goals and tasks, this question arises: What can the pilgrim rely on to do this job? How can the traveler proceed? On what horizon can the pilgrim stand within his or her self that will effect the emotional goals necessary to make one happy? The horizon on which the individual now struggles and grasps in darkness and suffering to stand is his or her own real and true self. Our sojourner leaves the self-concept as a frame of reference and embraces the real self as the source of perception…as his or her new reality, value, and possibility assumptions about self and world. This is a new habit and the birth of a good habit. The journey was made in darkness and in suffering. It was made in weakness, and as St. Paul has said, the results of the journey were such that he "gloried in his weakness" (2 Cor 12:9).

In proceeding toward formulating a spirituality for the traveler's emotional suffering in this experience, it would be good to expose the basic elements of the spiritual dynamics inherent here.

St. Paul was no stranger to suffering and weakness. His spirituality, his relationship with God, was enmeshed with suffering in his moving to God's will for him. To accomplish God's will for him, he encountered massive suffering. He rejoiced in this suffering because he knew he was moving with God into God. This suffering occurred in Paul's contact with the world. This weakness occurred in his own flesh from within. The cause was the environment from without. God used the world and Paul's own flesh to draw Paul to God's own love and bring Paul to full stature: personal freedom and love. Paul had to rely on God's strength and love and power in the suffering he encountered as he answered God's call. This suffering became so deep it rendered his own capacities impotent in accomplishing any significant reality changes. Paul walked this road in darkness, pain, and suffering. Paul relied on the Lord. The Lord responded, and Paul stood on a new horizon of being: God's very being. This is the source of Paul's freedom and love. He has a new horizon of being: the very being of God alone. This is the source of Paul's freedom and love: the presence of God as his horizon of being. Paul was drawn by God to do human feats that caused massive suffering and pain. As Paul traveled through this, he became aware of the presence of God's power with him. This freed Paul in a way never before possible for him. Paul came to freedom and love as a person. Paul thus said, "I rejoice in my weakness" (2 Cor 12:9).

St. John of the Cross speaks of the purification of the memory. He did not understand the purification of the memory from the radical perspective of the discovery of the unconscious as we know it today, simply because it was not available to him in his own day. The very meaning of an unconscious—that there exists in human beings a body of memories, a reservoir of experiences, that they are unaware of because these memories are so painful—this understanding was not available to John of the Cross. Human beings unconsciously repress memories. We now know that. Human beings do this because of the deep pain attached to, and residing in, these memories. They deny to this deep pain the access to their awareness. They do not want to remember these memories because of the deep pain of anger, sorrow, and unfulfilled need that these memories generate. These memories, these experiences, and the feelings resulting from them become unconscious to an individual's very self. This is the very meaning of the unconscious. The discovery of the unconscious was, as I have said, one of the greatest human achievements of the twentieth century, and the resultant method of revealing to individuals their own unconscious is one of the greatest contributions to the spiritual life to date.

The simplicity and enormity of this discovery was not available to St. John of the Cross in his time as it is to us today. Therapy reveals to individuals their own repressed memories and the pain involved and attached to those memories. The purification of one's memory is the discovery of one's unconscious. Discovering one's unconscious pain and working through it purify one's memory. We understand this "darkness" today as the dark journey into one's unconscious. The precision of the discovery of the unconscious and the methodology of therapy would indeed be a welcomed and enlightening element for John.

At the same time, St. John of the Cross is no stranger in this journey. He presents a spirituality of great darkness and suffering in moving from his former perceptions of God into the unknown. His experience of coming to know the Lord, his experience of coming to love with the love of God, his experience of coming to full stature constitutes a long journey to personal freedom and love in God. He presents this process of pain and darkness in his emotional and sensible capacities as he is forced to rely on his intellectual and volitional capabilities to live. He presents the ever deepening pain of the darkness put in his intellect and will as God induces aridity in his contemplative prayer life. Here he had to travel on, seeking and reaching out for God in complete suffering, pain, and darkness. This he did, and the Lord showed himself to him, becoming John's everything. The Lord became John's total source. God became the horizon on which John related to the world. The Lord became John's source of being and horizon of being. This freed John to such a degree that he could say, "Glad night." John was drawn by God to walk through the complete darkness of all of his capacities toward

God alone. In so doing, John realized that God was more powerful than all of his capabilities. John realized that God was with him even in darkness, pain, and suffering. God became John's horizon of being. This journey was made in darkness and in suffering. John had to leave his former habits of feelings, perceptions, and ideas about himself and about God for God alone. This journey was made in great suffering and darkness. In thus leaving the known for the unknown, John came to full personal freedom and love.

A spirituality arises from the dynamic elements presented by these two experiences. The Pauline notion of "weakness" and the Johanine notion of "darkness" coalesce in the action of God to bring a human being to full stature: reliance on God alone as one's source and horizon of being, personal freedom, and love! The process of incapacitating an individual's capabilities is the experience of weakness and darkness. For Paul and John, this experience of impotency in their capacities initiates a deeper growth culminating in an individual's reliance on a more powerful, freer, more loving reality: God. This experience of such complete suffering is one of moving from weakness to strength, from darkness to light, from the unknown to the known. This experience is the same for our traveler's struggle from false self-concept to real-self health. The incapacitating of the human capabilities of Paul and John and the resulting power of having God as the horizon and source of their being, of freedom and love, are mirrored in the incapacity of the traveler's false self-concept in effecting any qualitative life change for the real self and in his or her movement through this in psychotherapy to freedom and loving real-self relating. As Paul and John's human capacities were darkened and rendered ineffective, so also is the traveler's self-concept rendered ineffective. What the pilgrim has thought to be effective is now seen as ineffective. The traveler sees that the self-concept is not the real self and cannot effect real-self living. This is massive suffering for the pilgrim grasping on in darkness. The same rhythm and process is occurring here: the process of a darkness, the process of a weakness, the process of a journey from the known into the unknown, and the process of coming to a freedom as one moves continually forward. The experience of the weakness of Paul and the experience of the darkness of John speak deeply here to the traveler's struggle and psychotherapeutic suffering.

The suffering our Christian traveler goes through in moving toward real-self living is a weakness and a darkness like Paul and John's as they moved toward the same God, the same freedom, and the same love. It is different, however, in that the instrumentality, the arena of action between God and the traveler, is each one's conflict between a distorted self-concept life and a real-self life.

The instrumentality principally used by God in bringing St. Paul to God was the opposition and antagonism of the world and other human beings to the gospel. The instrumentality used by God with St. John of the Cross was his own prayer life of contemplation and meditation. The instrumentality used by God with our pilgrim traveler is his or her own false self-concept living. God, freedom, love, and the result remain the same. The way God draws a person respects his or her individual personhood.

Discussion Questions

Have you experienced the painful and dark journey of discovering your unconscious? Share with your group.

Have you experienced false self-concept behavior in yourself? How so?

Have you experienced the pain and darkness of knowing that you need to change but not knowing how to do it? Discuss.

Have you experienced the emergence of your real self from within? In what ways?

During this sometimes long journey in darkness, did you experience the presence, strength, and comforting grace of Christ calling you to move ahead in peace? Was this an experience of the shepherd guiding the sheep?

Is the purification of memory spoken of by St. John of the Cross better served by the methodology of psychotherapy? How?

Does the discovery of one's unconscious through therapy constitute coming to self knowledge? Discuss in your group.

CHAPTER FOURTEEN

Divine Union:
Identification with Christ

I would like to delve into the mystery of the identification of the experiences of St. Paul, St. John of the Cross, and our pilgrim traveler. In order to do this, I would like to appeal again to the experience of the early-sixteenth-century founder of the Society of Jesus, St. Ignatius of Loyola.

Here it would help to look at the final contemplation of St. Ignatius of Loyola in his Spiritual Exercises, a thirty-day individually directed retreat. This is entitled "The Contemplation to Attain the Love of God." St. Ignatius says:

Two things are to be noticed here:

The first is, that love ought to be found in deeds rather than words.

The second is, that love consists in mutual interchange on either side, that is to say, in the lover giving and communicating with the beloved what one has or can give, and on the other hand, in the beloved sharing with the lover, so that if the one have knowledge, honours, riches, they share it with the one who has them not, and thus the one share all with the other.[200]

St. Ignatius goes on to give us his first point in this contemplation: look at all the gifts received "of my creation, redemption, and particular gifts, dwelling with great affection on how much God our Lord has done for me."[201] He has the retreatant ask the question, "What am I doing for Christ?"[202]

In the second point for contemplation, Ignatius asks the retreatant to "consider how God dwells in creatures, in the elements giving them being, in the plants giving them growth, in animals giving them feeling, and in women and men giving them understanding, and in me giving me being, life, feeling, and causing me to understand."[203]

God gives us all of this so that we can give ourselves to each other, so that we can love each other, so that we can be thankful for ourselves and for each other.[204] God gives us all of this so that we can love God by loving each other. God gives us all of this to fulfill the Scripture: "Insofar as you did this to one of the least of these sisters and brothers of mine, you did it to me" (Matt 25:40). Here is the reality of identification.

In these words, the Creator God of the universe, Christ Jesus, has revealed the meaning of creation. You and I are not in charge of the meaning of reality. You and I do not make the meaning of reality or the definitions of reality. Only God does this. In these words of Jesus Christ, God has restructured the entire meaning of reality. All of the attempts we make to love ourselves and to love others are in reality attempts to love God and to respond to God. All of the seeking out, the searching, the attempts to untangle ourselves from crippling emotional blocks are attempts to "love in deed rather than words." All of our attempts to embark on the journey to free ourselves so that we can receive love and respond spontaneously are attempts to love by mutual sharing and interchange of what I have with what another has. This is love. This is love of God. This is loving. This is prayer. This is holiness. This is spiritual. This is the meaning of the spiritual life. Who says so? Jesus Christ! When He says, "Insofar as you did this to one of the least of these sisters and brothers of mine, you did it to me" (Matt 25:40).

God labors for us and with us in every relationship and in every reality in our lives to bring us to full stature, as St. Ignatius reveals in the third point of his "Contemplation to Attain the Love of God": "This is to consider how God works and labors for me in all creatures upon the face of the earth, that is, He conducts Himself as one who labors. Thus, in the heavens, the elements, the plants, in all, giving life and sensation."[205]

This Ignatian insight of identification is the product of his Spiritual Exercises, a considered pattern of biblical prayer extending for a period of approximately thirty consecutive days. Each day lived in silence is occupied by five hours of individual prayer. A spiritual director sees the individual making the Spiritual Exercises once or twice a day. The matter of their discussions is what goes on in the individual's prayer life: the hours of prayer. The fruit wished for as a result of making these Spiritual Exercises is the gift of contemplation in the Ignatian sense. The gift of contemplation given by Christ is the gift of the identification of one's life with Christ Jesus in his life. This gift of contemplation consists in placing oneself via one's imagination into a New Testament gospel scene of the life of Christ. One watches Jesus heal a leper, hears his words, feels the heat of the sun, touches the Lord himself.[206] As an individual prays in this fashion, moving consistently through the life of the Lord Jesus, the here-and-now life of the retreatant begins to come up. Christ brings up a retreatant's present life. The origin of this grace is the action of Christ himself. The faces of the people in one's own life come up. The circumstances of one's own life begin to emerge. The retreatant begins to receive from Christ a realization of an identification of his or her very own life with the life of Jesus in grace. As the Lord gives the gift of contemplation, the retreatant begins to see his or her own individual pain as Christ's pain, identifies the pain Christ lived through with pain that the retreatant is living through.[207] As the retreatant sees Jesus attempt to bring love into the world and free human beings, the retreatant is given by Christ to see his or her own efforts to bring love into the world, to be his or her very self, and to free human beings as the same as Christ's. There is an identification made with Jesus Christ and Christ's life as one and the same. Christ gives the graceful realization that one's own organic pain at bringing oneself and one's love and freedom into the world is identical with the effort and experience of Christ. It is the same reality. This is the gift of contemplation in the Ignatian sense: the gift of seeing one's own organic life as the same as the life and work and experience of Jesus Christ.

This gift of grace is that one sees the necessity to be oneself freely and lovingly as a religious reality. One now looks upon one's efforts of loving as holy and as a movement with God and toward

God with Christ. One sees one's work, pain, suffering, and effort to be one's real self in the world as the same work, pain, suffering and effort of Christ. This is one event.

This is a prayer made in and with one's very being. It is a prayer of one's flesh, one's emotion, one's intellect, and one's being. It is a prayer of one's real self. It is a prayer of one's person. One sees one's real-self movement—to be and to share one's real self—as a movement toward God as was Christ's. This then becomes living the same spiritual life as Christ with Christ. This is the very meaning of the spiritual life.

Our traveler's emotional struggle to understand the vague feeling of something being wrong, the traveler's struggle to free the self from the outer-directed self-conceptual defense habits, to look at his or her own real-self feelings, and to express them is a struggle to love and to give oneself to others and therefore to God. "Insofar as you did this to one of the least of these sisters and brothers of mine, you did it to me" (Matt 25:40). It is an attempt to share with others one's greatest gift: oneself. It is an attempt to thank others and God and to stand in a general freedom toward all things. This is prayer. This is prayer of the heart and mind, a prayer of emotion and intellect, a prayer of the flesh in the flesh, and a prayer of body and spirit. The historical definition of prayer is to lift one's heart and mind to God. Every element of the experience of lifting one's real self to one's self and to others is therefore prayer and therefore holy according to the design of the Creator of the universe, Christ Jesus. Every element of our traveler's experience is with Christ and for Christ. It is the spiritual life. Christ alone defines the meaning of all things. Christ alone can define the meaning of the spiritual life.

The Christian person in our contemporary society moves toward God by relating to the world and by relating with the human beings he or she lives with. God is using the instrumentality of the world and other human beings to touch and call out the real self of each Christian traveler. God is drawing our traveler to Christ Jesus with Christ Jesus.

Christ calls to human beings to come out of safe and protected life comforts and habits and to trust in God. This is a call to come to full stature: personal freedom in the world before God and in the presence of God's people.

Discussion Questions

The historical definition of *prayer* is "the lifting of one's heart and mind to God." Christ says, "Insofar as you did this to one of the least of these sisters and brothers of mine, you did it to me" (Matt 25:40). Does this mean, then, that every move you make to share who you really are with another person is prayer? Discuss.

Is this the very meaning of holiness? Why?

Is there an identification in you with regard to our traveler and the life of Christ? Share with your group.

Is there an identification in you with regard to your experience and the life experience of Christ? Discuss.

Is being your real self freely in the world the very meaning of holiness? Why?

CHAPTER FIFTEEN

Spiritual Indwelling

The instrumentality the Lord chooses to bring our Christian traveler in emotional suffering to real-self living and to a general freedom and love toward all things is the world and other human beings. What Christ uses to draw our traveler to God alone is his or her personality and emotional conflict: the pain rising within upon reality contact. Reality contact with the world and other people, relationships of love and fear and anger, sorrow and need, and reality contact with life's tasks mean involvement and interaction. This means receiving and giving, being impressed, and reacting and responding. This contact with the world causes organic emotional pain, torment, and affliction. This is darkness for our Christian traveler's personality. Christ Jesus in wisdom is using the world God created to call to the suffering traveler, the pilgrim, to draw the person to love and freedom. This is a dark road. Yet it is the same road that St. Paul traveled on. It is the same road that St. John of the Cross traveled on. It is the same road that St. Ignatius of Loyola traveled on. Our suffering pilgrim is moving to real-self freedom and sharing his or her real self. This is as Jesus did and for those Jesus says are himself: other human beings. This is toward God with God and in God. Our Christian traveler sees with the eyes of faith that he or she is moving toward God with God. The Christian traveler sees with the eyes of faith how his or her own struggle to love is the same struggle that Jesus endured and lived out. With faith the Christian suffering emotional pain sees the presence of God here, calling one out to be and share one's real self, to love. It is the element of faith here that opens the real nature of this journey. The Christian sufferer's faith in Jesus as Lord and Creator focuses his or her ability and capacity to perceive the presence of God as the beginning, the road, and the omega point of this dynamic suffering in life. The Christian sufferer sees that the struggle is a spiritual movement toward God. Emotional suffering and resolution are spiritual direction and the spiritual life.[208]

The spirituality of St. John of the Cross contributes a very refined methodology to this road of emotional suffering and resolution: the movement from the known to the unknown as darkness. The exploration, the isolation, and the meaning of darkness in St. John of the Cross have been the underlying methodological tool to make clear and to see the emotional struggle for what it really is: an attempt to be one's real self, to function fully, to love, and therefore prayer. The spirituality of St. Paul contributed the methodology of meeting, facing, and overcoming obstacles in the world, triumphing over them, and rejoicing in them. Although St. Paul was baptized into Christianity miraculously through a vision of Christ, he was confirmed by his struggles with the world to bring Christ to women and men. This highlighted the role of the world and brought it into the picture of spirituality as an integral element. The spirituality of St. Ignatius exposed the presence of God as Creator in all organic life. These elements are the anatomy of the spiritual life. St. John of the Cross's notion of "darkness" and St. Paul's notion of "weakness" and St. Ignatius's notion of "seeing God in all things" bring to light the dynamic dimensions of the spiritual life.[209]

The whole emotional struggle is one of moving from the known to the unknown, of attempting to accept one's humanness, one's vulnerability, and one's needs and, by accepting them and identifying with them, finding joy and love interacting with the world. All of these elements coalesce in a view of the emotional struggle as the grasping, the moving, and the traveling of a person organically, emotionally, and intellectually toward his or her Creator and Lord, who is Love. All of these elements coalesce in the view of a journey to uncover the unconscious conflict that is crippling a person as, wholly and ultimately, engineered by the hand of God through the instrumentality of reality contact. All of these elements coalesce in the view of this journey as a God-given gift of freedom and love rejoicing in the darkness left behind. All of these elements coalesce in the view of the joy of being able to share love and receive and respond emotionally as "the freedom of the children of God" (Rom 8:21).

Only in God can we relate fully with ourselves and with each other. God's effect upon us reaches to the very marrow of our being and existence.

The path of St. Paul and St. John of the Cross toward God is a guide for our pilgrim. Their path is an example, a paradigm, a model-image, and there is here a deeper reality that the gift of the Spiritual Exercises of St. Ignatius Loyola enlightens. There is the reality of identification with our pilgrim's own darkness and weakness. St. Paul and St. John of the Cross left familiar, secure, and comfortable patterns and habits of perceiving themselves, the world, and God as they worked through unfamiliar, insecure, and painful "nights" to a deeper reality: relying on God alone. This resulted in freedom and love. The Christian pilgrim suffering emotional conflictual pain leaves the familiar, secure, and known patterns of false self-conceptual perceptions of self, the world, and God. The pilgrim moves through an unfamiliar, insecure, and painful "night" to a much deeper reality of living: his or her real-self living. This results in true freedom and love. There is an identification here between Paul, John, Ignatius, Christ, and the Christian traveler suffering emotional conflictual pain. This is the level of identification. This is union in identification.

From the way Paul and John and Ignatius speak and act concerning their love of themselves, others, and God, it is clearly evident that the effects of God's love for them and their reliance on God alone have penetrated deeply their emotional lives. They are free and loving human beings. Whether either St. Paul or St. John of the Cross had experienced emotional conflictual pain as the typical and common traveler of our society does today is not as important as the fact that at some time they faced some of these experiences, as all human beings exhibit some of these or similar characteristics at some time in their lives. The important thing to note here, however, is the action of God upon them. It is important that the effect of God's presence in their lives reached into their emotional lives, bringing them to a freedom toward all things and a deep love and respect for all things, as God is free and is loving and respectful toward God's own creation. God brings Paul and John through vision, the world, and prayer to this freedom and love. God brings the Christian traveler suffering emotional conflictual pain to freedom and love through a process with a coun-selor-guide. The task is to see the presence and power of God in the organic power of the real world and in the power of real selves call-ing the Christian traveler's real self into real living.

God wants the emotionally suffering Christian traveler to live the spiritual life: to go through this process to be one's real self in reality. God is not going to deal with everyone as God did with Paul and John. We use them to identify more clearly the presence of God in the encounter of the emotionally suffering Christian with a coun-selor-guide, in their interaction.

In this light, then, the Christian traveler suffering emotional conflictual pain sees his or her own movement to free the real self to love and relate to others as living the spiritual life: a movement toward God, the same God of St. Paul, St. John of the Cross, and St. Ignatius of Loyola. The same God has a hand on the emotion-ally suffering traveler, dealing with him or her as with the mystic saints. God is disarming the traveler of defenses through the instru-mentality of God's real-world, reality contact, just as God disarmed St. Paul through his world and St. John of the Cross through his prayer. The real self of the traveler is the result. Our pilgrim is now free and loving, and God says, "Now you are who I made you to be." The real selves of Paul and John stand free and loving, and God says, "You are who I made you to be." Christ Jesus and one's real self, free and loving, are enough. One's Creator and one's cre-ated self, free and loving, are enough, as Ignatius would say. God wants free and loving human beings. God wants us to share our free personal selves with one another. This is movement toward God. This is prayer. "Insofar as you did this to one of the least of these sisters and brothers of mine, you did it to me" (Matt 25:40). In these words God has identified the emotional psychological experi-ence and the spiritual experience as one. God in these words has identified the emotional psychological and the spiritual dynamic as one. In these words the God and Creator of all reality has restruc-tured the meaning of all things, saying that every movement we make toward our sisters and brothers is a movement toward God. In these words the God and Creator of all reality has identified every movement we make toward our sisters and brothers as prayer. In this is born the realization that our psychological lives and our spiritual lives are one event. In this is born the identification of psychological counseling and spiritual direction as being one event. The spiritual life is one movement. God in Christ Jesus has here revealed that prayer is one reality: love.

The spiritual life involves deep emotional suffering. The spiritual life identifies as the very meaning of holiness human love, human loving, and all of the movements a human being suffering emotional conflictual pain makes to reach out and love one's self and other human beings. The spiritual life identifies as a movement to love Jesus Christ each organic movement and decision a suffering human being makes to be one's self and to share one's self with another human being. The spiritual life identifies each movement and decision a suffering human being makes to be one's real self and to share one's real self with another human being as holy, as prayer, as a movement and a decision to share oneself with God...to love God.

The spiritual life identifies this suffering in St. Paul as weakness and in St. John of the Cross as darkness. The suffering a person endures while moving, through a painfully familiar habit of perceiving oneself and the outside world, to an unknown yet deeper and real perception of who one really is is the spiritual life. The darkness and weakness are good and a rich human spiritual reality.

As our pilgrim moves through the suffering present in traveling the spiritual road of emotional conflicts and resolution, the Pauline and Johannine and Ignatian notion of the hand of God orchestrating this darkness and weakness exposes the presence of God's hand in his or her life.

The spiritual life is the seeing of the presence of God in all things. The Ignatian notion of seeing this, and that love is shown in deeds, identifies our traveler's decisions and movements to be free and loving as prayer: movement toward God.

Paul and John arrive at freedom and love. Our Christian traveler suffering emotional pain arrives at freedom and love. It is God drawing our pilgrim toward God through God's own creation with and through the counselor-guide's observations. The same God, acting here and drawing the emotionally suffering Christian pilgrim, drew Paul and John of the Cross and Ignatius.

The spiritual life is the process of identifying Christ's presence and caring love in the experience of emotional suffering, of identifying God's hand and presence in all of creation. Christ wants God's children to share who they are with one another. Resolving emotional issues frees an individual to do that.[210]

Christ emerges in one's spiritual life as wanting to set one free. God's presence and loving action call out through and within one's emotional suffering for resolution. This is Christ's call to set God's captives free.

The spiritual life is one of human emotional and psychological struggle. The spiritual life is a movement from darkness to light, of struggle and of final success, of moving through the unknown to the known, through fear to ultimate love.

The spiritual life exposes the spiritual power to free a person. The spiritual life exposes the care and love of God for us in God's own creation. The spiritual life reveals that Christ is present in the world, working for God's own creatures to free and love them. The spiritual life lays bare God's love present in the world. The spiritual reality in the struggle is the presence of Christ in God's own creation. As the Apostle John put it, "God is love" (1 John 4:8).

Discussion Questions

Is your struggle to love the same struggle that Christ lived out in his life? How so?

Do you recognize that only in God can you fully relate to your self, others, and the world? Why?

How does God reach the very marrow of your being?

Do you see your own movement to free yourself and to love others with your real self as a movement toward God? In what ways?

Is sharing your real joy, need, sorrow, self-love, and anger with your sisters and brothers prayer? Discuss.

How does God disarm you and draw you into God's very self?

Psychological counseling and spiritual direction are one and the same movement. Discuss.

"God is love" (1 John 4:8). Discuss.

Notes

1. All scripture references are from *The Jerusalem Bible* (London: Darton, Longman & Todd, 1985).

2. Karen Horney, M.D., *Neurosis and Human Growth* (New York: W. W. Norton, 1992), p. 158.

3. Ibid.

4. Robert A. Harper, *Psychoanalysis and Psychotherapy* (Englewood Cliffs, N.J.: Prentice-Hall, 1959), p. 156.

5. Thomas à Kempis, *The Imitation of Christ* (London: Penguin Group, 2000), pp. 21–28.

6. Alphonsus Rodriguez, S.J., *The Practice of Perfection and Christian Virtues, vol. 1*, trans. Joseph Rickaby (Chicago: Loyola University Press, 1929), p. 3.

7. Ibid., p. 95.

8. Ibid., p. 131.

9. Ibid., p. 185.

10. Ibid., p. 421.

11. Ibid., p. 467.

12. Alphonsus Rodriguez, S.J., *The Practice of Perfection and Christian Virtues, vol. 2*, trans. Joseph Rickaby (Chicago: Loyola University Press, 1929), p. 3.

13. Ibid., p. 165.

14. Ibid., p. 355.

15. Ibid., p. 456.

16. Alphonsus Rodriguez, S.J., *The Practice of Perfection and Christian Virtues, vol. 3*, trans. Joseph Rickaby (Chicago: Loyola University Press, 1929), p. 446.

17. Ibid., p. 473.

18. John of the Cross, *The Collected Works of St. John of the Cross*, trans. Kieran Kavanaugh, O.C.D., and Otilio Rodriguez, O.C.D. (Washington, D.C.: ICS Publications, Institute for Carmelite Studies, 2001), p. 73.

19. Ibid., p. 297.

20. Teresa of Avila, *The Collected Works of St. Teresa of Avila*, vol. 2. trans. Kieran Kavanaugh, O.C.D., and Otilio Rodriguez, O.C.D. (Washington, D.C.: ICS Publications, Institute for Carmelite Studies, 2001), p. 283.

21. Evelyn Underhill, *The Mystics of the Church* (New York: Schocken Books, 1971), p. 179.

22. John Welch, O.Carm., *Spiritual Pilgrims: Carl Jung and Teresa of Avila* (New York: Paulist Press, 1982), p. 21.

23. Teresa of Avila, op. cit., pp. 283, 297, 304.

24. Ibid., pp. 316, 335, 359.

25. Ibid., pp. 283, 288.

26. Ibid., p. 297.

27. Ibid., p. 304.

28. Welch, op.cit., p. 76.

29. Teresa of Avila, op. cit., p. 316.

30. Ibid., p. 335.

31. Ibid., p. 427.

32. Welch, op. cit., p. 100.

33. Ibid., p.104.

34. Pierre Teilhard de Chardin, S.J., *The Divine Milieu* (London: Collins; New York: Harper and Brothers, 1959), pp. 7–8.

35. Ibid., pp. 55–56.

36. Ibid., p. 8.

37. Ibid., pp. 95–96.

38. Ibid., p. 99.

39. Alfred Adler, *What Life Should Mean to You* (New York: G. P. Putnam's Sons, 1958), p. 120.

40. Erik H. Erikson, *Childhood and Society* (New York: W. W. Norton, 1963), p. 247.

41. Alfred Adler, *Problems of Neurosis* (New York: Harper and Row, 1964), p. 31.

42. Alfred Adler, *Social Interest* (New York: Capricorn Books, 1964), pp. 220–221.

43. Ibid., p. 220.

44. Abraham Maslow, *Principles of Abnormal Psychology: The Diagnosis of Psychic Illness* (New York: Harper and Row, 1941), p. 414.

45. Otto Fenichel, M.D., *The Psychoanalytic Theory of Neuroses* (New York: W. W. Norton, 1945), p. 117.

46. Alfred Adler, *Understanding Human Nature* (Greenwich, Conn.: Fawcett Publications, 1954), p. 42.

47. Horney, *Neurosis and Human Growth*, p. 158.

48. Maslow, op. cit., p. 237.

49. Adler, *What Life Should Mean to You*, p. 121.

50. Karen Horney, M.D., *Our Inner Conflicts* (New York: W. W. Norton, 1993), p. 41.

51. Jean Piaget and Barbel Inhelder, *The Psychology of the Child* (New York: Basic Books, 1969), p. 121.

52. Horney, *Our Inner Conflicts*, p. 100.

53. Ira Progoff, *Depth Psychology and Modern Man* (New York: Julian Press, 1959), p. 156.

54. Horney, *Our Inner Conflicts*, p. 37.

55. Ibid.

56. Horney, *Neurosis and Human Growth*, p. 110.

57. Horney, *Our Inner Conflicts*, p. 47.

58. Karen Horney, M.D., *The Neurotic Personality of Our Time* (New York: W. W. Norton, 1991), p. 137.

59. Fenichel, op. cit., p. 141.

60. Karen Horney, M.D., *New Ways in Psychoanalysis* (New York: W. W. Norton, 1992), p. 136.

61. Flanders Dunbar, M.D., *Synopses of Psychosomatic Diagnoses and Treatment* (St. Louis: C. V. Mosby, 1948), p. 396.

62. Fenichel, op. cit., p. 143.

63. Horney, *Neurosis and Human Growth*, p. 160.

64. Fenichel, op. cit., p. 193.

65. Ibid., p. 187.

66. Horney, *Our Inner Conflicts*, p. 140.

67. P. M. Lichtenstein, M.D., and S. M. Small, M.D., *A Handbook of Psychiatry* (New York: W. W. Norton, 1941), pp. 116–125.

68. Horney, *Our Inner Conflicts*, p. 121.

69. Ibid., p. 130.

70. Horney, *The Neurotic Personality of Our Time*, p. 81.

71. Ibid., p. 81.

72. Robert W. White, *The Abnormal Personality* (New York: Ronald Press, 1956), p. 38.

73. Horney, *Our Inner Conflicts*, p. 31.

74. Karen Horney, *Neuroses and Human Growth*, p. 110.

75. Horney, *The Neurotic Personality of Our Time*, pp. 85–86.

76. Ibid., p. 101.

77. Ibid., p. 230.

78. Justin Aronfreed, *Conduct and Conscience* (New York: Academic Press, 1968), p. 245.

79. Horney, *Neurosis and Human Growth*, p. 64.

80. Ibid.

81. James A. Knight, M.D., *Conscience and Guilt* (New York: Appleton-Century-Crofts, 1969), p. 95.

82. Horney, *The Neurotic Personality of Our Time*, pp. 234–235.

83. Knight, op. cit., p. 95.

84. Horney, *The Neurotic Personality of Our Time*, pp. 232–233.

85. Ibid., p. 232.

86. Ibid., p. 222.

87. Ibid., p. 239.

88. Horney, *Neurosis and Human Growth*, p. 122.

89. Horney, *Our Inner Conflicts*, p. 111.

90. Horney, *Neurosis and Human Growth*, p. 23.

91. Ibid., p. 25.

92. Horney, *Our Inner Conflicts*, p. 101.

93. Heinz L. Ansbacher and Rowena R. Ansbacher, eds., *The Individual Psychology of Alfred Adler* (New York: Harper & Row, 1995), p. 14.

94. Alfred Adler, *The Practice and Theory of Individual Psychology* (New York: Harcourt, Brace, 1932), p. 101.

95. Adler, *What Life Should Mean to You*, p. 51.

96. Alfred Adler, *The Science of Living* (Garden City, N.Y.: Doubleday, 1968), p. 6.

97. Adler, *Social Interest*, p. 149.

98. Ibid.

99. Adler, *The Science of Living*, p. 27.

100. Adler, *Problems of Neurosis*, p. 149.

101. Ibid., p. 87.

102. Alfred Adler, *The Neurotic Constitution* (New York: Moffat, Yard, 1916), p. 38.

103. Adler, *Problems of Neurosis*, pp. 31–32.

104. Alfred Adler, *Social Interest,* p. 146.

105. Adler, *The Neurotic Constitution*, p. 52.

106. Adler, *Social Interest*, p. 148.

107. Ibid., p. 244.

108. Ibid., p. 147.

109. Adler, *The Science of Living*, p. 7.

110. Adler, *Understanding Human Nature*, pp. 139–140.

111. Adler, *What Life Should Mean to You*, pp. 221–222.

112. Horney, *Our Inner Conflicts*, p. 27.

113. Robert A. Harper, *Psychoanalysis and Psychotherapy* Englewood Cliffs, N.J.: Prentice-Hall, 1959, p. 9.

114. Horney, *Our Inner Conflicts*, p. 114.

115. Horney, *New Ways in Psychoanalysis*, p. 305.

116. Karen Horney, M.D., in "What Does the Analyst Do?" *Are You Considering Psychoanalysis?* (New York: W. W. Norton, 1992), p. 189.

117. Ibid., p. 191.

118. Ibid., p. 194.

119. Ibid., p. 196.

120. Horney, *New Ways in Psychoanalysis*, p. 207.

121. Ibid., p. 208.

122. Horney, *Neurosis and Human Growth*, p. 160.

123. Horney, *Our Inner Conflicts*, p. 102.

124. Ibid., p. 209.

125. Adler, *Understanding Human Nature*, p. 36.

126. Adler, *Social Interest*, pp. 275–276.

127. Ibid., p. 147.

128. Adler, *The Practice and Theory of Individual Psychology*, p. 41.

129. Ibid., p. 3.

130. Ansbacher and Ansbacher, op. cit., pp. 408–409.

131. Adler, *The Practice and Theory of Individual Psychology*, p. 42.

132. Adler, *The Education of Children* (Chicago: Gateway Editions, 1930), p. 150.

133. Adler, *The Theory and Practice of Individual Psychology*, p. 42.

134. Adler, *Social Interest*, p. 208.

135. Adler, *What Life Should Mean to You*, p. 73.

136. Horney, *Our Inner Conflicts*, p. 104.

137. Bede Rigaux, *The Letters of St. Paul* (Chicago: Franciscan Herald Press, 1968), p. 51.

138. Ibid., pp. 54–55.

139. A. Robert and A. Feuillet, *Introduction to the New Testament* (New York: Desclée, 1965), p. 381.

140. Joachim Jeremias, "The Key to Pauline Theology," *Expository Times* 76 (October 1964): 29.

141. Robert and Feuillet, op. cit., p. 381.

142. *The Interpreter's Bible*, vol. 10 (New York: Abingdon Press, 1956), p. 409.

143. Raymond E. Brown, Joseph A. Fitzmyer, and Roland E. Murphy, *The Jerome Biblical Commentary* (Englewood Cliffs, N.J.: Prentice-Hall, 1968), p. 289.

144. Xavier Leon-Dufour, *Dictionary of Biblical Theology* (New York: Desclée, 1967), p. 515.

145. Robert and Feuillet, op. cit., p. 382.

146. Rigaux, op. cit., p. 61.

147. Jeremias, op. cit., p. 270.

148. John L. McKenzie, *Dictionary of the Bible* (Milwaukee: Bruce, 1965), p. 650.

149. Crisogono de Jesus, O.C.D., *The Life of St. John of the Cross* (New York: Harper and Brothers, 1958), p. 44.

150. Ignatius of Loyola, *The Spiritual Exercises of St. Ignatius: Based on Studies in the Language of the Autograph*, trans. Puhl, Louis J., S.J. (Chicago: Loyola Press, 2001), p. 12.

151. John of the Cross, op. cit., pp. 295–296.

152. Underhill, *The Mystics of the Church*, p. 181.

153. John of the Cross, "The Ascent of Mount Carmel," op. cit., p. 74.

154. Ibid., p. 75.

155. Ibid.

156. Evelyn Underhill, *Mysticism* (New York: E. P. Dutton, 1961), p. 395.

157. John of the Cross, "The Ascent of Mount Carmel," op. cit., p. 140.

158. Ibid.

159. Ibid., 141.

160. Ibid.

161. Ibid.

162. John of the Cross, "The Dark Night," op. cit., p. 313.

163. Ibid., p. 314.

164. Ibid., p. 315.

165. Ibid.

166. Ibid.

167. Ibid., p. 316.

168. William Johnston, *The Still Point* (New York: Fordham University Press, 1970), p. 98.

169. John of the Cross, "The Dark Night," op. cit., p. 336.

170. Ibid.

171. Ibid., p. 332.

172. Ibid., p. 333.

173. Underhill, *Mysticism*, p. 353.

174. John of the Cross, "The Dark Night," op. cit., p. 340.

175. Ibid., p. 341.

176. Ibid., p. 342.

177. Ibid., p. 346.

178. Ibid., p. 353.

179. Ibid.

180. John of the Cross, "The Living Flame," op. cit., p. 578.

181. Ibid., pp. 578–579.

182. Ibid., p. 649.

183. Underhill, *Mysticism*, p. 397.

184. Ibid., p. 396.

185. John of the Cross, "The Dark Night," op. cit., p. 346.

186. Underhill, *Mysticism*, p. 388.

187. John of the Cross, "The Dark Night," op. cit., pp. 295–296.

188. Underhill, *The Mystics of the Church*, p. 181.

189. Luis Gonzales de Camara, *St. Ignatius' Own Story*, trans. William J. Young, S.J. (Chicago: Loyola University Press, 1950), pp. 22–23.

190. Alexander Reid Martin, M.D., "Why Psychoanalysis?" in *Are You Considering Psychoanalysis?* ed. Karen Horney, M.D. (New York: W. W. Norton, 1992), p. 18.

191. Horney, *Our Inner Conflicts*, pp. 110–111.

192. John B. Enright, "An Introduction to Gestalt Techniques," in *Gestalt Therapy Now*, ed. Joen Fagan and Irma Lee Shepherd (New York: Harper and Row, 1971), p. 108.

193. Horney, *Our Inner Conflicts*, p. 47.

194. Ibid.

195. Robert Plutchik, *The Emotions: Facts, Theories, and a New Model* (New York: Random House, 1967), p. 151.

196. Horney, *Our Inner Conflicts*, p. 56.

197. Jean-Pierre de Caussade, S.J., *Abandonment to Divine Providence*, trans. John Beevers (New York: Doubleday, 2001), p. 82.

198. Horney, *Our Inner Conflicts*, p. 238.

199. John of the Cross, op. cit., p. 69.

200. Ignatius of Loyola, op. cit., p. 101.

201. Ibid., pp. 101–102.

202. Karl Rahner, S.J., *Spiritual Exercises* (New York: Herder and Herder, 1966), p. 273.

203. Ignatius of Loyola, op. cit., p. 102.

204. William A. M. Peters, S.J., *The Spiritual Exercises of St. Ignatius: Exposition and Interpretation* (Jersey City, N.J.: Program to Adapt the Spiritual Exercises, 1968), p. 163.

205. Ignatius of Loyola, op. cit., p. 103.

206. Peters, op. cit., p. 85.

207. Ibid., p. 146.

208. Raymond Bailey, *Thomas Merton on Mysticism* (Garden City, N.Y.: Doubleday, 1975), p. 195.

209. Underhill, *Mysticism*, pp. 183–184.

210. David E. Roberts, *Psychotherapy and a Christian View of Man* (New York: Charles Scribner's Sons, 1951), p. 7.

Bibliography
and Suggested Reading

Abrams, Jeremiah, ed. *Reclaiming the Inner Child*. New York: Penguin Putnam, 2000.

Adler, Alfred. *The Education of Children*. Chicago: Gateway Editions, 1930.

———. *The Neurotic Constitution*. New York: Molfat, Yard, 1916.

———. *The Practice and Theory of Individual Psychology*. New York: Harcourt, Brace, 1932.

———. *Problems of Neurosis*. New York: Harper and Row, 1964.

———. *The Science of Living*. Garden City, N.Y.: Doubleday, 1968.

———. *Social Interest*. New York: Capricorn Books, 1964.

———. *Understanding Human Nature*. Greenwich, Conn.: Fawcett Publications, 1954.

———. *What Life Should Mean to You*. New York: G. P. Putnam's Sons, 1958.

Adorno, Theodor W., *Aesthetic Theory*. Minneapolis: University of Minnesota Press, 1999.

Amodeo, John. *The Authentic Heart*. New York: John Wiley and Sons, 2001.

Ansbacher, Heinz, and Rowena Ansbacher, eds. *The Individual Psycholoqy of Alfred Adler*. New York: Harper & Row, 1995.

Aronfreed, Justin. *Conduct and Conscience*. New York: Academic Press, 1968.

Bailey, Raymond. *Thomas Merton on Mysticism*. Garden City, N.Y.: Doubleday, 1975.

Barry, William, S.J. *Letting God Come Close: An Approach to the Ignatian Spiritual Exercises*. New York: Paulist Press, 2001.

———. *With an Everlasting Love*. New York: Paulist Press, 1999.

Billy, Dennis J. *The Way of a Pilgrim*. Liguori, Mo.: Liguori Publications, 2000.

Breemen, Peter van, S.J., *The God Who Won't Let Go*. Notre Dame, Ind.: Ave Maria Press, 2001.

Brown, Deborah A., ed. *Christianity in the 21st Century*. New York: Crossroad, 2000.

Brown, Raymond E., S.S., Joseph A. Fitzmyer, S.J., and Roland E. Murphy, O. Carm. *The Jerome Biblical Commentary*. Englewood Cliffs, N.J.: Prentice-Hall, 1968.

Bulman, Raymond F. *The June of the Millennium*. New York: Orbis Books, 2000.

Burt, Donald X. *The River: Reflections on the Times of Our Lives*. Collegeville, Minn.: Liturgical Press, 1998.

Byron, William, S.J. *Answers from Within*. New York: Macmillan, 1998.

Camara, Luis Gonzales de. *St. Ignatius' Own Story*. Translated by William J. Young, S.J. Chicago: Loyola University Press, 1956.

Caussade, Jean-Pierre de, S.J. *Abandonment to Divine Providence*. New York: Doubleday, 2001.

———. *A Treatise on Prayer from the Heart*. St. Louis: Institute of Jesuit Sources, 1988.

Crisogono de Jesus, O.C.D. *The Life of St. John of the Cross*. New York: Harper and Brothers, 1958.

Dister, John E., S.J. *A New Introduction to the Spiritual Exercises of St. Ignatius*. Collegeville, Minn.: Liturgical Press, 1993.

Dunbar, Flanders, M.D. *Synopsis of Psychosomatic Diagnosis and Treatment*. St. Louis: C. V. Mosby, 1948.

Egan, Harvey D., S.J. *Ignatius Loyola the Mystic*. Collegeville, Minn.: Liturgical Press, 1991.

Enright, John B. "An Introduction to Gestalt Techniques," in *Gestalt Therapy Now*, edited by Joen Fagan and Irma Lee Shepherd. New York: Harper and Row, 1971.

Erikson, Erik H. *Childhood and Society*. New York: W. W. Norton, 1963.

Fabing, Robert, S.J. *The Eucharist of Jesus: A Spirituality for Eucharistic Celebration*. Portland, Oreg.: Catholic Press, 1986.

———. *Experiencing God in Daily Life: The Habit of Reflecting on Love, Joy, Need, Fear, Sorrow, and Anger*. Portland, Oreg.: Catholic Press, 1991.

————. *Real Food: A Spirituality of the Eucharist.* New York: Paulist Press, 1994.

Fenichel, Otto, M.D. *The Psychoanalytic Theory of Neurosis.* New York: W. W. Norton, 1945.

Fiand, Sr. Barbara, S.M.D. de N. *Prayer and the Quest for Healing.* New York: Crossroad, 1999.

Ford-Grabowsky, Mary, ed. *Sacred Voices.* San Francisco: Harper Collins Publications, 2002.

Forest, Jim. *The Ladder of the Beatitudes.* New York: Orbis Books, 1999.

Gallagher, Winifred. *Spiritual Genius.* New York: Random House, 2001.

————. *Working on God.* New York: Random House, 1999.

Gelpi, Donald L., S.J. *Varieties of Transcendental Experience: A Study in Constructive Postmodernism.* Collegeville, Minn.: Liturgical Press, 2000.

Green, Thomas H., S.J. *The Friend of the Bridegroom: Spiritual Direction and the Encounter with Christ.* Notre Dame, Ind.: Ave Maria Press, 2000.

Groeschel, Benedict J., C.F.R. *Spiritual Passages.* New York: Crossroad, 2000.

Guardini, Romano. *The Art of Praying.* Manchester, N.H.: Sophia Institute Press, 1994.

Hahn, Kimberly. *Life Giving Love.* Ann Arbor, Mich.: Servant Publications, 2001.

Harper, Robert A. *Psychoanalysis and Psychotherapy.* Englewood Cliffs, N.J.: Prentice-Hall, 1959.

Harrington, Daniel, S.J. *Why Do We Suffer: A Scriptural Approach to the Human Condition.* Franklin, Wisc.: Sheed and Ward, 2000.

Healey, Charles J., S.J. *Christian Spirituality.* New York: Alba House, 2000.

Herbison, Priscilla, J. *God Knows We Get Angry.* Notre Dame, Ind.: Sorin Books, 2002.

Heyns, R. W. The *Psychology of Personal Adjustment.* New York: Dryden Press, 1958.

Horney, Karen, M.D. *Feminine Psychology.* New York: W. W. Norton, 1993.

————. *Neurosis and Human Growth*. New York: W. W. Norton, 1991.

————. *The Neurotic Personality of Our Time*. New York: W. W. Norton, 1991.

————. *New Ways in Psychoanalysis*. New York: W. W. Norton, 1995.

————. *Our Inner Conflicts*. New York: W. W. Norton, 1993.

————. "What Does the Analyst Do?" in *Are You Considering Psychoanalysis?* New York: W. W. Norton, 1992.

Ignatius of Loyola. *The Spiritual Exercises*. Westminster, Md.: Newman Bookshop, 1943.

————. *The Spiritual Exercises of St. Ignatius: Based on Studies in the Language of the Autograph*. Translated by Louis J. Puhl, S.J. Chicago: Loyola Press, 2001.

The Interpreter's Bible. Vol. 10. New York: Abingdon Press, 1956.

Jeremias, Joachim. "The Key to Pauline Theology" *Expository Times* 76 (October 1964): 27–30.

John of the Cross. *The Collected Works of St. John of the Cross*. Translated by Kieran Kavanaugh, O.C.D., and Otilio Rodriguez, O.C.D. Washington, D.C.: ICS Publications, Institute for Carmelite Studies, 2001.

Johnson, Luke Timothy. *Living Jesus*. San Francisco: Harper Collins, 2000.

————. *Religious Experience in Earliest Christianity: A Missing Dimension in New Testament Studies*. Minneapolis: Augsburg Fortress, 1988.

Johnston, William, S.J. *Mystical Theology*. New York: Orbis Books, 2000.

————. *The Still Point*. New York: Fordham University Press, 1970.

Johnston, William, S.J., ed. *The Cloud of Unknowing and the Book of Privy Counseling*. New York: Doubleday Image, 1996.

Jones, Timothy. *Awake My Soul: Practical Spirituality*. New York: Doubleday, 2000.

Keating, Thomas, O.C.S.O. *Awakenings*. New York: Crossroad, 1999.

————. *Open Mind Open Heart*. New York: Continuum, 2002.

Kelly, Joseph, F. *The Problem of Evil in Western Tradition.* Collegeville, Minn.: Liturgical Press, 2002.

Kelly, Tony, C.Ss.R. *Behold the Cross: Meditations for the Journey of Faith.* Liguori, Mo.: Liguori Publications, 1999.

Kempis, Thomas à. *The Imitation of Christ.* London: Penguin Group, 2000.

Kennedy, Michael, S.J. *Eyes on the Cross: A Guide for Contemplation.* New York: Crossroad, 2001.

―――. *Eyes on Jesus.* New York: Crossroad, 2000.

King, Ursula. *Christian Mystics.* New York: Paulist Press–Hidden Spring, 2001.

―――. *Pierre Teilhard de Chardin.* New York: Orbis Books, 1999.

Kirvan, John. *Silent Hope.* Notre Dame, Ind.: Sorin Books, 2001.

Knight, James A., M.D. *Conscience and Guilt.* New York: Appleton-Century-Crofts, 1969.

Kodell, Jerome. *Twelve Keys to Prayer.* Collegeville, Minn.: Liturgical Press, 2000.

Leon-Dufour, Xavier. *Dictionary of Biblical Theology.* New York: Desclée, 1967.

Lichtenstein, P. M., M.D., and S. M. Small, M.D. *A Handbook of Psychiatry.* New York: W. W. Norton, 1943.

Martin, Alexander Raid, M.D. "Why Psychoanalysis?" in *Are You Considering Psychoanalysis?* edited by Karen Horney, M.D. New York: W. W. Norton, 1946.

Martin, Ralph. *Hungry for God.* San Francisco: Ignatius Press, 2000.

Maslow, A. H., and Bela Mittelmann, M.D. *Principles of Abnormal Psychology: The Diagnosis of Psychic Illness.* New York and London: Harper and Brothers, 1941.

Mayes, Andrew D. *Spirituality of Struggle.* New York: Paulist Press, 2002.

McKenzie, John L. *Dictionary of the Bible.* Milwaukee: Bruce, 1965.

Merton, Thomas. *Contemplation in a World of Action.* Notre Dame, Ind.: University of Notre Dame Press, 1988.

Naranjo, Claudio, "Present-Centeredness: Technique, Prescription, and Ideal," in *Gestalt Therapy Now,* edited by Joen Fagan and Irma Lee Shepherd. New York: Harper and Row, 1971.

The New Jerusalem Bible. London: Darton, Longman & Todd, 1985.

O'Collins, Gerald, S.J. *Christology: A Biblical, Historical, and Systematic Study of Jesus Christ*. Oxford: Oxford University Press, 2000.

Olin, John C., ed., and Joseph F. O'Callaghan, S.J., trans. *The Autobiography of Ignatius Loyola: With Related Documents*. New York: Fordham University Press, 1993.

Peters, William A. M., S.J. *The Spiritual Exercises of St. Ignatius: Exposition and Interpretation*. Jersey City, N.J.: The Program to Adapt the Spiritual Exercises, 1968.

Piaget, Jean, and Barbel Inhelder. *The Psychology of the Child*. New York: Basic Books, 1969.

Piper, John. *A Hunger for God: Desiring God through Fasting and Prayer*. Wheaton, Ill.: Crossway Books, 1997.

Plutchik, Robert. *The Emotions: Facts, Theories, and a New Model*. New York: Random House, 1967.

Progoff, Ira. *Depth Psychology and Modern Man*. New York: Julian Press, 1959.

Rahner, Karl, S.J. *Spiritual Exercises*. New York: Herder and Herder, 1966.

Rigaux, Beda. *The Letters of St. Paul*. Chicago: Franciscan Herald Press, 1968.

Robert, A., and A. Feuillet. *Introduction to the New Testament*. New York: Desclée, 1965.

Roberts, David E. *Psychotherapy and a Christian View of Man*. New York: Charles Scribner's Sons, 1951.

Rodriguez, Alphonsus, S.J. *The Practice of Perfection and Christian Virtues*. Translated by Joseph Rickaby. 3 vols. Chicago: Loyola University Press, 1929.

Rogers, Carl R. *Psychotherapy and Personality Change*. Chicago: University of Chicago Press, 1954.

Rohr, Richard. *Everything Belongs: The Gift of Contemplative Prayer*. New York: Crossroad, 2000.

Ruffing, Janet K., R.S.M. *Spiritual Direction*. New York: Paulist Press, 2000.

Silf, Margaret. *Inner Compass: An Invitation to Ignatian Spirituality*. Chicago: Loyola Press, 1999.

Stinissen, Wilfred. *The Gift of Spiritual Direction*. Liguori, Mo.: Liguori Publications, 2000.

Sweet, Leonard. *Postmodern Pilgrims: First Century Passion for the 21st Century Church*. Nashville: Broadman & Holman, 2000.

Taylor, Barbara Brown. *When God Is Silent*. Lyman Beecher Lectures on Preaching, 1997. Cambridge, Mass.: Cowley Publications, 1998.

Teilhard de Chardin, Pierre, S.J. *The Divine Milieu*. New York: Harper and Brothers, 1959.

————. *Heart of Matter*. New York: Harcourt Brace Jovanovich, 1978.

————. *Hymn of the Universe*. New York: Harper and Row, 1970.

————. *The Phenomenon of Man*. New York: Harper and Brothers, 1959.

Teresa of Avila. *The Collected Works of St. Teresa of Avila*. Vol. 2. Translated by Kieran Kavanaugh, O.C.D., and Otilio Rodriguez, O.C.D. Washington, D.C.: ICS Publications, Institute for Carmelite Studies, 2001.

Tetlow, Joseph A., S.J. *Ignatius Loyola—Spiritual Exercises*. New York: Crossroad, 2000.

Underhill, Evelyn. *Mysticism,* New York: E. P. Dutton, 1961.

————. *The Mystics of the Church*. New York: Schocken Books, 1971.

Vallee, Gerard. *The Shaping of Christianity*. New York: Paulist Press, 1999.

Vanier, Jean. *Becoming Human*. New York: Paulist Press, 1998.

Wallen, Richard. "Gestalt Therapy and Gestalt Psychology," in *Gestalt Therapy Now*, edited by Joen Fagan and Irma Lee Shepherd. New York: Harper and Row, 1971.

Welch, John., O.Carm. *Spiritual Pilgrims: Carl Jung and Teresa of Avila*. New York: Paulist Press, 1982.

White, Robert W. *The Abnormal Personality*. New York: Ronald Press, 1956.